GOD BEHIND BARS

THE AMAZING STORY OF **PRISON FELLOWSHIP**

JOHN PERRY

FOREWORD BY **CHARLES COLSON**

W PUBLISHING GROUP
A Division of Thomas Nelson Publishers
Since 1798

www.wpublishinggroup.com

GOD BEHIND BARS

Published by W Publishing Group, a Division of Thomas Nelson, Inc., P.O. Box 141000,
Nashville, Tennessee, 37214.

W Publishing Group books may be purchased in bulk for educational, business,
fundraising, or sales promotional use. For information, please e-mail
SpecialMarkets@ThomasNelson.com.

All Scripture quotations, unless otherwise indicated, are taken from The Holy Bible,
New International Version (NIV). Copyright © 1973, 1978, 1984, International Bible
Society. Used by permission of Zondervan Bible Publishers.

Library of Congress Cataloging-in-Publication Data

Perry, John, 1952–
  God behind bars : the amazing story of Prison Fellowship / John Perry.
     p. cm.
  Includes bibliographical references.
  ISBN-10: 0-8499-0014-X
  ISBN-13: 978-0-8499-0014-3
  1. Prison Fellowship. 2. Church work with prisoners—United States.
I. Title.
  BV4340.P46 2006
  259'.5—dc22

                                          2006013001

Printed in the United States of America
06 07 08 09 QW 9 8 7 6 5 4 3 2 1

This book is dedicated to Tom Phillips, who by God's grace set Chuck Colson on the pathway to Christ; to Doug Coe, Harold Hughes, Graham Purcell, and Al Quie, steadfast Christian brothers who so faithfully and so well shared the journey; to the men and women who since have carried the light of Jesus into the darkest corners of the earth; and to those God is preparing even now to lift His torch higher still.

Table of Contents

Foreword

As I look back on the thirty years of Prison Fellowship's ministry, I consider myself the most blessed man alive.

I am profoundly grateful to God that He has allowed me to see hundreds of thousands of prisoners and their families transformed by the grace of Jesus Christ, to witness countless Christian volunteers mobilized to carry the love of Christ into America's darkest dungeons, and to see the church affirming God's sovereignty over all of life, embracing a thoroughly biblical worldview as it engages our modern culture.

I know beyond a shadow of a doubt that none of this was my doing. In fact, God had to work in my heart to get me on board.

When I was released from prison in 1975, I really did not want to start a prison ministry. I did have thoughts of returning to Washington and using my connections to do something to straighten out the mess that was—and, sadly, still is—America's prison system. But beginning a national prison ministry was not what I envisioned.

My wife, Patty, and I had decided we wanted to spend more time with our family. We had just been through two brutal years of Watergate and my own imprisonment. We had been beaten to a pulp. It was time to live a quiet life.

I entertained some very interesting and potentially lucrative proposals to go into business. But during that first year out of prison, I began to sense that God had put me in prison for a purpose, and that I had to do something with that experience. Still, I was reluctant, for Patty's sake, to begin any major undertaking.

It was exactly thirty years ago this summer that I realized God had been at work in Patty's heart as well. We were vacationing at a friend's home on the Oregon coast. While we were sitting there one evening, reading books, listening to the waves coming in off the Pacific, she leaned toward me and asked, "You're really wanting to go into ministry, aren't you?" I told her yes, that's what I thought God wanted me to do. So she looked at me and said, "Well, I'm OK with that; let's go."

That started the ministry. I really sensed God's hand on me then, and I have sensed His hand on me—and on this great movement called Prison Fellowship—every step of the way. His hand had to be on us, or this ministry never would have survived some of the challenges. There were times when things looked bleak indeed—whether as the result of our own missteps, or circumstances beyond our control—and I wondered if Prison Fellowship would endure.

But as author John Perry will show you throughout the pages of this book, God had a plan for Prison Fellowship. Again, none of the great things we've done in this ministry are a result of our own genius or strategizing. It was simply God at work.

Take Angel Tree, for instance. Mary Kay Beard, a gun moll on the FBI's most wanted list, spent years in the Alabama state prison system. We hired her as Prison Fellowship's state director in Alabama. In 1982, she set up a Christmas tree in a Montgomery shopping mall so people would could buy gifts for the children of prisoners. I heard about it later. People come up to me today and tell me what a great idea I had to start Angel Tree. I tell them, "I didn't even know about it!"

Many things along the way have been like this. Our first in-prison seminar took place because a warden in Oxford, Wisconsin, decided that we couldn't take any of his inmates out of prison to participate in our Washington Discipleship Seminar. Instead, the warden challenged us to bring our program inside his prison. So we found thirty volunteers, organized them, took them into the prison, and had a weeklong seminar. Some ninety prisoners participated, with a third of them coming to Christ in during that week. Today, the In-Prison Seminar is the backbone of our ministry behind bars.

God did that. We didn't figure it out.

Nor did we figure out Operation Starting Line. That started when Aaron Johnson, the Secretary of Corrections in North Carolina, stood up in front of a room full of Prison Fellowship staff members, stretched out his arms and told us, "I am the man from Macedonia" (a beautiful reference to Acts 16:9) and begged us to come and minister in all of his state prisons. We didn't think we could do it. But we also didn't think we could ignore what seemed to be a divinely inspired plea. That was back in 1991. And today, nearly thirty other Christian ministries have joined us in this nationwide prisoner-evangelization effort. To date, nearly six hundred thousand prisoners have attended Operation Starting Line events and have heard the Good News of Jesus Christ; tens of thousands have been led to Christ.

All of this is to say that the true history of Prison Fellowship is the history of God at work, which is why I trust that John Perry enjoyed researching and writing this book. On the other hand, I know for a fact that this was not an easy task. It would be impossible to write a purely chronological history of Prison Fellowship. Throughout the course of our history, there have been so many twists and turns, starts and stops and starts again. How it all fits together is only apparent through the lens of God's sovereignty.

I am often asked, for instance, why the Wilberforce Forum—which teaches Christian worldview—is part of Prison Fellowship. By the late

1970s, I began to realize that we were swimming upstream when it came to the crime problem. Despite the amazing transformation we were witnessing in the lives of individual prisoners as they came to Christ, the problem of crime was getting worse and worse. Prison populations weren't shrinking, they were soaring!

As I studied the problem, I came across a study on the causes of crime by Stanton Samenow and Samuel Yockelson. At the beginning of their study, they held to the conventional wisdom that poverty, environment, broken families, racism, and so forth caused crime. But what they concluded after seventeen years of studying prisoners, was that crime was caused by people "making wrong moral choices." That certainly matched my experience and the experiences of the people I got to know in prison.

Then in 1981, I read *Lectures on Calvinism*. Based on the Stone Lectures on biblical worldview given at Princeton by Abraham Kuyper, the great Dutch theologian who later became prime minister of Holland, that book genuinely transformed my life.

There's a very easy explanation of what *worldview* is, because we all have one. It is one's basic understanding of how the world works and how one fits in. Where did we come from? Why is there sin and suffering? What can we do to fix the mess we're in? What's our purpose in life? How we answer those questions—or simply ignoring them—will go a long way toward determining how we live our lives. In other words, our worldview matters.

So then I began to realize that is really what's wrong with the crime problem. Most most people have a faulty worldview, and. Their their behavior reflects their worldview.

My thinking was confirmed in the mid-1980s when I read a study by professors James Q. Wilson (then at Harvard) and Richard Herrnstein, who concluded that crime is caused by a lack of moral teaching during the morally formative years. They found no correlation between crime and race, poverty, or anything else people usually associate as a cause of crime.

What does that tell us? As moral teaching that should be passed on from generation to generation is disregarded, crime goes up.

By 1991 we began "BreakPoint" radio, applying Christian world-view commentary to news and trends. And by 1999 we launched the Wilberforce Forum, named after English Parliamentarian William Wilberforce, whose monumental efforts led to the end of the slave trade in the British Empire. (I should add that I'm grateful to John Perry for including in this book the enormous influence of Wilberforce on my life and on Prison Fellowship!)

This ministry, which started out in simple obedience to God's call, not having any grand design, has grown into an international ministry that evangelizes and lives out the gospel on the one hand, and speaks truth in love to the culture on the other.

Perhaps the most gratifying thing about this ministry is the people God has raised up to make it possible. When I started the ministry, a lot of leaders told me I'd never get support working in the prisons because evangelicals didn't care about prisoners. God has certainly confounded that conventional wisdom. Today there's an army of people across America who share this vision to take the gospel to the neediest people in our society. Along with the prisoners who have been trans-formed, it is folks like that—folks like you—who have given their lives to this work who encourage me the most. To the staff and the volun-teers and the many friends and supporters who have made this min-istry possible, I want to take this opportunity to tell you how much, from the bottom of my heart, I appreciate you.

I find it such a privilege that I have lived long enough to see God bring all of this to fruition. *Soli Deo Gloria.*

Charles Colson
Washington, D.C.
April 2006

Acknowledgments

A story as broad and far reaching as this one depends on many hands and many voices for a proper telling. I'm grateful to Chuck Colson, who graciously suggested that I write a history of Prison Fellowship, and who encouraged me at every turn; to Matt Jacobson, my friend long before he was my agent, who first put the pieces together; to Greg Daniel, associate publisher at W Publishing, who has been a champion of this book from the beginning and an unfailing source of grace and encouragement; and to Thom Chittom, whose editorial skills were a tremendous addition.

At Prison Fellowship, David Carlson supplied me with every fact I asked for and patiently advised me through many months of research; Val Merrill has been a rock of organizational stability; Bessie Cool knows the phone number of every important person on the planet and let me peek at her list as circumstances required.

Those who were there in the beginning kindly shared their thoughts: Al Quie, Gordon Loux, Neal Jones, Paul Kramer, Lisa Stackpole, and others. Thanks also to those who have led the charge through the years: David Cauwels, Peter Ochs, Dallen Peterson, Dois Rosser, Ellen

Vaughn, Claude Rhea, Tom Pratt, Mark Earley, Alan Terwilleger, Pat Nolan, Steve Varnam, Karen Strong, and their many partners in ministry. Thanks to Bob Woodward for taking time to speak with me even though, we now know, he was then on the cusp of new controversy over the identity of Watergate's famous Deep Throat.

At the InnerChange Freedom Initiative facility in Newton, Iowa, I'm grateful to program directors Dan Kingery and Chris Geil, and to Warden Terry Mapes, who kept his promise to answer questions as long as I wanted to ask them. I also owe a debt of thanks to the men incarcerated there who spoke with me. They are some of the greatest Christians I've ever met. I wish I could share the stories of every one of them—maybe someday I will.

Of the historical references I've used, Prison Fellowship publications, particularly *Jubilee* newsletters, were especially helpful because of the excellent work of Becky Beane and others on the PF writing team. For a more general look at the subject, I leaned heavily on *The Oxford History of the Prison* and *With Liberty for Some* by Scott Christianson. I've done my best to be complete and accurate in my facts and citations; any errors or omissions are entirely my own.

Only God's providence could have pulled this book together over so long a time and so many sources. It's my prayer that it will honor Him as Prison Fellowship has done well for so long. And may God bless Chuck Colson, his co-laborers, and their work for many more years to come.

John Perry
Nashville
Memorial Day, 2006

[CHAPTER 1]
Broken Vessels

The story of the most successful prison reform and prisoner rehabilitation program in American history began at a miserable moment
of national shame and ends some time in the future. Its principle figure—young, rich, immensely talented, and at the height of his personal and political influence—tumbled from one of the most powerful
positions in world affairs to one of the most hopeless and despised: a
convicted felon.

Prison destroys many people. It breaks prisoners both innocent and
guilty, dangerous and harmless; their spouses and children, who
endure physical loss, cultural rejection, and often financial collapse;
even those counselors and corrections officers who finally see and feel
more anger, fear, and hopelessness than they can bear. But prison did
not break Charles W. Colson, former special counsel to President
Richard Nixon. By the time Colson reported to federal authorities in the
summer of 1974 to begin serving his sentence, there was nothing break-
able left in him. A life-changing experience the year before had shattered the old Colson; the new one faced incarceration with steady
resolve and brave anticipation. The old Colson, in fact, could have

avoided imprisonment altogether, while the new one felt honor bound to uphold standards greater than any government statute.

Life behind bars prompted Colson to look at the whole philosophy of prison as punishment from an entirely new angle. Examining closely the conditions he and others lived under, he worked through his thoughts on a series of questions, jotting down ideas on yellow legal pads like the ones he used in the White House to make notes during his conversations with the president. What was the purpose of imprisonment? What did it achieve? What were the alternatives? What rights did a prisoner have, and what rights should he have?

Like most Nixon Republicans, Colson had been "tough on crime," favoring harsh sentences and limits on parole to get lawbreakers off the streets for good. When rioting inmates armed themselves and took several hostages at Attica Prison in the summer of 1971, New York Governor Nelson Rockefeller had ordered state troopers to storm the doors. After the shooting finally stopped, thirty-one prisoners and nine guards lay dead. Colson encouraged the president to call Governor Rockefeller and congratulate him for hanging tough. "No doubt about it, Mr. President," Colson had said, gesturing out the windows of the Oval Office. "Our people out there have had enough of being soft on criminals."

A few years later Colson would become a criminal himself, and realize firsthand that the system wasn't so soft after all. One fellow inmate of Chuck's had gone to court accused of minor tax violations, made a remark that infuriated the judge and consequently drew an eighteen-month sentence. Suddenly his once-comfortable family had no father, husband, or breadwinner, and he had a criminal record. Another man, a successful self-made business owner, unknowingly cashed a stolen check for eighty-four dollars. He paid six thousand dollars in legal fees and still spent six months in prison, costing him six months' income on top of everything else. A number of the convicts in Colson's prison dormitory were illiterate, unable to understand the charges against them, their prospects for parole, or any of the legal details of their cases—including their rights as inmates.

Most of all Colson saw the sense of hopelessness that engulfed prisoners behind bars. Except for meals and roll call several times a day, prisoners were on their own to pass the time any way they could. Most of them had no prison job, no hobby they could pursue, no evident interests. Colson wrote later of the men in his dorm who spent their days on their cots in a zombie-like state, dozing or staring at the ceiling. Some worked for hours on menial tasks like shining a belt buckle. They walked at a slow, shuffling pace. "Like an invasion of locusts," Colson observed, "the empty hours eat away at a man's very being. Soon there is near-total disorientation: staring at the clock, its hands never moving; losing track of time and place."

In 1974 when Charles Colson was incarcerated, there were about two hundred thousand inmates in America's state and federal prisons. Today there are more than 2.2 million, an elevenfold increase. These men and women (94 percent of prisoners are men) are largely ignored and forgotten by society. But what happens to them in prison is important to everyone because most of them will eventually be released, and the way they were treated on the inside affects their behavior on the outside. For millions of us it gets personal: one day we'll find ourselves sharing the same employer, the same neighborhood, in some cases even the same apartment building with ex-cons.

About two hundred thousand prisoners are either serving life sentences or will die before their terms are up. The other two million will be back on the street sooner or later. Will prison have made them better people less likely to commit crimes? Will it have dealt decisively with the drug addiction and dysfunctional families most prisoners struggle with? Will it have taught them a trade so they can support themselves and their dependents? Will it steer them away from people and places associated with past criminal behavior, reducing the temptation to fall into old habits?

In spite of their years behind bars and regardless of whatever government-mandated programs they've been through—drug rehab, anger management, family relationships, or others from a long list of possibilities—the majority of ex-offenders are also future offenders. Far from being rehabilitated, prisoners often sharpen their lawbreaking skills and make new contacts on the inside; they become a greater threat to public safety when they get out than when they went in. Within three years, two-thirds of them will be rearrested. And they are only the ones who get caught.

The second time through the penal system these convicts will take more mandatory classes, learn more criminal skills (or teach theirs to newcomers), and make more connections among their fellow inmates and gang members. Some criminals repeat this cycle ten times over the course of their careers, with first offenders adding fresh fodder along the way.

The cost to society of continuing this flawed system is staggering. Current laws and sentencing requirements have led to more people being locked up for longer periods, driving America's prison population to a historic high. Building enough new cells to hold them all is straining government budgets nationwide. Prison construction is booming, with each new cell costing taxpayers about $100,000. Food, clothing, infirmary care, and other expenses add about $23,000 per inmate annually. And that's only part of the system cost. Unreformed ex-offenders are on the outside committing new crimes, raising the costs of law enforcement, security, property damage, theft, and medical treatment thousands of dollars. On top of all that is the intangible cost of crime to the victims, their families, the families of offenders, and the community at large.

As one warden with almost thirty years of criminal justice experience recently observed, "The prison system is broken and everybody knows it." Yet despite compelling evidence of an enormously expensive failure, the whole operation rolls along very much the same year after year. Why?

One reason is bureaucratic inertia. Creative, dedicated, energetic men and women work for America's prison systems, but those systems are too often wary of them. The bureaucratic mind-set holds fast to policy and precedent. Like other government organizations such as school districts or the postal service, state and federal corrections systems are staffed by people trained to follow instructions. Success is measured by how well workers stick to the rules. As one prison official explained, "You're rewarded for how well you follow procedures. The thing you want most of all is not to screw up." Innovation and creative thinking equate with risk; doing it the way it's always been done is the safe path to favorable performance reviews and secure progress up the career ladder. Why take a chance on a reprimand by thinking outside the box when it's so easy just to do what you're told? As in the military, directives are there to be followed, not questioned.

A second reason to hang on to a failed prison system is that changing it carries high political risk. Politicians who write the laws, and judges and district attorneys who enforce them, know that being "tough on crime" earns them points with the voters. One of the most obvious ways to prove they're tough is to put more criminals behind bars. So mandatory sentencing laws discourage plea bargains and shorter prison terms, and three-strikes-and-you're-out statutes lock up habitual offenders for decades. The assumption is that the more convicted wrongdoers we lock up, the safer the community is.

A third barrier to prison reform is that for most citizens, prisons and prisoners are completely off the radar. They're out of the public eye, often far from populated areas, and most people don't think much about them one way or the other. With so many demands on public resources, allotting time and money to investigating prison improvements is not a priority. Criminals, the reasoning often goes, are the dregs of society living somewhere far away, and certainly less worthy of tax dollars than schools, hospitals, police departments, firehouses, highways, libraries, and almost anything else. It's what sociologist

Phillip Slater called "the toilet assumption." This, he explained, is believing "that unwanted matter, unwanted difficulties, or unwanted complexities will disappear if they are removed from our immediate field of vision."

For many years, a fourth impediment to improving America's prison system has been that there was evidently no alternative to it. For all the faults in the traditional approach, it at least has the advantage of familiarity. Our prison bureaucracy and legal system are deeply invested in it. With no other viable possibilities on the horizon, systemic inertia, political risk, and public attitude are not necessarily the prime limiting factors to exploring other ways to run prisons and rehabilitate prisoners. Rather the biggest problem is having no radically new directions to explore. With nothing worth championing, there has been no reason to risk a promotion, pension, or election by stepping out of long-held comfort zones.

Charles Colson and the organization he founded, Prison Fellowship Ministries (PF), have now spent thirty years developing an alternative approach to prison and prisoner reform. PF has grown from a shoestring operation in a Washington, D.C.–area basement to the largest and most influential force in history for reshaping society's thinking about prisons, punishment, rehabilitation, restitution, justice, and the causes of crime.

Even though Prison Fellowship has a presence in every prison in the United States and nearly more than one hundred countries around the world, many who praise its work know little about the dramatic events that gave it birth and saw it through the dark valleys and promising peaks of the past three decades. High-profile politicians, religious leaders, show business personalities, sports heroes, and other public figures have played various roles in these events—some helped, some hurt, and others dragged their feet unsure how far PF should go.

Literally millions of men, women, and children know the story firsthand. These are the prisoners, ex-prisoners, their families, prison

officials, politicians, crime victims, law enforcers, volunteers, and supporters who have been touched in some way by PF. Still others will
remember Charles Colson as a player in the high drama of the Watergate
affair, which led to President Nixon's resignation on August 9, 1974.

But for people under forty who have never been directly affected by
crime, the name "Charles Colson" or "Prison Fellowship" might bring
nothing immediately to mind. In the end though, they're the ones who
may be most amazed at how PF's radical approach to crime and punishment has begun a transformation of the entire criminal justice system, not just in how criminals are punished but upstream in dealing
with root causes of criminality. The ministry's conclusions are obvious
to some and startling to others, the remedy even more so. Yet the
results of PF's work show current success and future promise beyond
anything that has been done before.

In the beginning, Charles Colson could scarcely have imagined his
own prison term would spark a chain of events leading to such a legacy.
Two years to the day after President Nixon resigned his office, Colson
was one of a small group gathered around the seed of an idea they
dared to hope might change prisons for the better. None of them had a
career in the corrections industry, though two of them had themselves
been prisoners. They held few resources for the task ahead and had
little to guide them beyond the convictions of their hearts.

Prison Fellowship Ministries started with the simple observation
that rehabilitating a criminal is impossible if the criminal doesn't want
to change. For the short-term he can be coerced by threats, rewards, or
punishment into taking a course, making a promise, or signing a sheet of
paper that pleases the parole board or fulfills some procedural mandate.
But if a man wants to abuse drugs, steal from his employer, or beat his
girlfriend, no rehab program or classroom training will keep him from it.

The only way to reshape an offender's behavior pattern for good,
this group believed, was not to impose changes from the outside, but to
kindle the desire to change from within.

In the face of skeptics and criticism, Prison Fellowship began putting its theory, already tested on a handful of prisoners, into practice on a wider scale. Its curriculum generated a remarkable transformation: true repentance, rehabilitation, and a desire to live a new, law-abiding life. There was transformation taking place even among career offenders, thugs, and murderers who were considered hopeless within the penal system.

The Fellowship insisted that this transformation from within was not on account of anything it had done, but came instead from the grace of God through Jesus Christ. Colson and his team claimed no power for themselves; rather, they were broken vessels used by God to achieve His purposes. Plenty of hard-boiled observers on both sides of the bars had their doubts. In the beginning critics could argue that PF was just another time-consuming community outreach program that inconvenienced the security staff. Some insisted it was another chance for bored inmates to take advantage of hapless do-gooders. Others questioned Colson's motives, wondering if it was just an attempt from a disgraced former Washington insider to burnish his public image. The critics could argue furthermore that Christianity was complete hokum. But after a while they couldn't argue with the results.

Three years earlier, Chuck Colson would have been an unlikely champion of either Christianity or prison reform. On the contrary, he had clawed his way to the very pinnacle of the Washington power structure, thanks in part to a reputation for ruthless efficiency—getting things done even if it meant "running over his own grandmother."

CHAPTER 2

Genesis

Charles Colson had admired Richard Nixon since their first meeting during President Dwight Eisenhower's reelection campaign in 1956. Nixon was Eisenhower's vice president and running mate, and Colson was a young, ambitious, and promising congressional staffer, one of the rising stars on Capitol Hill. At twenty-four, he already had an impressive track record.

Chuck Colson was an only child, born in 1931 to parents of immigrant stock. His father's family was from Sweden, his mother's from England. Growing up during the darkest years of the Depression, he remembered seeing block-long lines at the soup kitchen near his house in a Boston suburb. His father, Wendell, set an example by working hard for his family, putting his college plans on hold after his own father died. In order to provide in such lean times, Wendell took a bookkeeping job in a meatpacking plant at thirty-two dollars a week. Going to night school, he finally earned a law degree at age forty.

Chuck established high standards for himself early in life and worked hard to achieve them. He took summer jobs starting when he was eleven years old to help out with prep school tuition. He graduated in 1949 as valedictorian, was president of the student body, captain of the debate team, editor of the school newspaper, and voted most likely to succeed. Chuck turned down a full scholarship to Harvard because he thought the Harvard men who ran Boston's legal establishment were conceited and haughty, turning up their noses at his working-class father and his middle-class clients. Instead, Chuck accepted an ROTC scholarship to Brown University in Providence, Rhode Island.

In June 1953, Colson graduated "with distinction" from Brown; the same day he married a local beauty named Nancy Billings and then shipped out for Marine Corps basic training. He was disappointed not to get his lieutenant's commission before the Korean War ended. Soon his unit shipped out to Guatemala in support of a covert CIA mission to overthrow that country's pro-Communist president. Their orders were to wait aboard offshore transports in case CIA-trained Guatemalan exiles needed help repossessing their homeland.

Standing at the rail looking out at the dark shoreline, Lieutenant Colson wondered what it would be like to give an order that would get other men killed. He could never remember thinking seriously about religion before, even though he did go to church once in a while. But looking up at the stars he felt sure that God was out there somewhere. Where was He? Here was one young soldier on the deck of a ship surrounded by untold galaxies of creation. Chuck had no idea what would happen tomorrow, but he believed God was in control. He prayed more fervently and sincerely than he'd ever prayed before, somehow sure that God would watch over him.

After daybreak the marines got word that the invasion had been a success; they wouldn't have to join the fighting. For days afterward, that feeling Lieutenant Colson had of God's presence lingered with him—it had seemed so real! But it soon faded away as Colson sailed back to the United States, then on to an assignment in Puerto Rico. After completing his active duty in the Corps, Colson, his wife, and their new son moved to Washington, where Chuck enrolled in George Washington University Law School.

He entered a junior management training program sponsored by the government and soon landed a staff position with an assistant secretary of the navy. A year or so later, Chuck was offered a position as Republican Senator Leverett Saltonstall's executive secretary, the number two position in the office. Colson had only been on the Massachusetts senator's staff a few months when Saltonstall asked him to help write a speech for the Republican National Convention, nominating Vice President Richard Nixon for a second term.

Nixon was a hard-charging fighter who gained national recognition for his high-profile role in fingering Alger Hiss, formerly an editor at *Time* magazine, as a Communist spy. He was famous too for the "Checkers" speech, a nationally televised rebuttal of charges that he had benefited personally from campaign contributions, though, he insisted, he would keep the gift of a dog named Checkers no matter what anybody said.

Colson and Nixon met for the first time when Colson delivered a draft of the speech to the vice president's office. The young messenger walked in to find Vice President Nixon seemingly doing a dozen things at once: talking on the phone, dictating a letter, speaking with a visitor, and giving directions to various members of his staff. Colson handed over the speech, marveling at how smoothly Nixon added another task to all the rest, and how incisive and well-considered his questions and comments on the speech were.

It was the unlikely beginning of a historic friendship in American politics. Though separated by half a generation in age, the two men had important experiences and characteristics in common. They were both veterans (Nixon was in the navy) and from modest circumstances. They were patriots. They were social conservatives. And Colson admired the vice president's sharp elbows when it came to dealing with opponents and adversaries. Nixon had been elected to the U.S.

Senate in 1950 after mounting a searing personal attack on his oppo-
nent, Helen Gahagan Douglas, a former film actress married to
Hollywood star Melvyn Douglas. Hammering away at her connections
with "pinkos" in the movie business, Nixon insisted that the choice
between Douglas and himself was "simply the choice between freedom
and state socialism."

By 1960 Colson had become Senator Saltonstall's chief of staff,
graduated from law school, and joined the American Bar Association.
During Saltonstall's reelection effort that year, Colson acquired a taste
for Nixon-style campaigning. Massachusetts' junior senator, John F.
Kennedy, was the Democratic presidential nominee running against
Nixon. Colson believed that the key voting bloc in the senate race
would be Irish Democrats. If they went for Saltonstall, he'd be reelected; if not, he'd lose. He convinced six prominent Democratic Irish
leaders in Boston to sign a letter supporting Kennedy and Saltonstall.
Then he rented rooms in a fleabag hotel and had Republican volunteers address the letters to everyone in the Boston phone book with an
Irish-sounding name—three hundred thousand listings in all.

The Nixon camp was furious when they learned that Saltonstall
had seemingly aligned with the opposition to take advantage of
Kennedy's popularity. Unaware of Colson's scheme, the senior senator
had continued to support Nixon in his speeches. After the dust settled,
Saltonstall won his race but Nixon lost the presidency by a whisker in
the national count, defeated overwhelmingly in Massachusetts thanks
to JFK's home-state popularity.

Colson was admired as the mastermind behind Saltonstall's victory. The Boston chamber of commerce voted him one of the Ten
Outstanding Young Men of 1960. But in spite of the accolades for his
political skills, Chuck decided to leave Capitol Hill and open a law
practice. He set up shop in Washington representing the New England
Council, a trade lobbying group. Within only a few years he was one of
the most successful and well-connected lawyers in the city. Unusual for

a Republican, Colson formed close and cordial ties with labor unions and trade associations through the connections his practice generated.

While his business career was on the rise, his life at home was falling apart. After ten years of marriage, the only thing he and Nancy had in common was their three children, Wendell, Christian, and Emily. She cared nothing for politics or the Washington social circle, and gradually husband and wife drifted apart. Though they remained friends, it became clear that they couldn't go on as a family. To avoid a long and potentially embarrassing court hearing in Washington, they got a Mexican divorce. Less than three months later, Colson married a former staffer from Senator Saltonstall's office named Patricia Hughes.

Patty was a Catholic and her church did not recognize Chuck's divorce, so the two held a civil ceremony at the army chapel near Arlington Cemetery. In spite of his best efforts, Chuck could not find a way around the church's disapproval. For a while he studied Catholicism with the same intensity he studied every other challenge in his life. "But my divorce appeared an insurmountable barrier to the blessing of her church," he wrote later, "and in time, I dropped it."

Nixon and Colson had kept in touch off and on through Nixon's second vice presidential term, his close and controversial loss to Senator Kennedy in 1960, and his stinging defeat in the California governor's race of 1962. While the Nixon star seemed to sink, Colson's rose steadily higher. During Nixon's subsequent years in the political wilderness, he and Colson remained in contact. When Nixon ran for president again in 1968 against formidable odds, Colson's sharp intellect and good relationships with the unions made him a valuable asset to the president's top advisory team, the "key issues committee." Highly competitive and determined to win, Colson was not above bending a few rules to secure his objective.

As a member of the committee, Colson secretly wrote a letter to three thousand Wall Street heavyweights over Nixon's signature, criticizing President Lyndon Johnson's proposed changes in securities regulations. Depending on how the reader interpreted it, it could also have been a veiled promise from Nixon not to implement those proposals if he were elected. The letter was harshly criticized on the Senate floor. Colson denied a report in *The Wall Street Journal* that he had written it. By Election Day, the storm had died down.

Nixon won the presidency by half a million votes, and Chuck Colson returned full time to his law practice. But soon offers started coming in to work for the new Republican administration. He had his choice of a job in the Transportation Department or as assistant secretary of state for congressional relations. What he really wanted, however, was a seat at President Nixon's inner circle. Before long he got the call he was waiting for: a direct invitation from the president to be his liaison to unions and other outside interest groups. He would be one of three special counsels to the president.

Though it was one of the most powerful jobs in the world, it was far from one of the highest paid. Colson would have to give up a salary of $200,000 a year, plus a car and driver, to work in the White House for $36,000. But serving as the president's personal advisor was too good to pass up. It would make Chuck Colson one of the most important and influential men anywhere. And once he finished his stint in the White House, he could make more money than ever as a member of Washington's most prestigious network of insiders. On November 3, 1969, Colson reported for his first day of work in the Nixon White House.

Officially, all the presidential special counsels worked under Nixon's chief of staff, H. R. Haldeman, a former advertising executive whose father had contributed to Nixon's congressional campaigns. After a few weeks on the job, Colson concluded that there were plenty of eager and well-meaning people around the president, but most of them were inexperienced and unfocused. They didn't know how to take advantage of the vast resources of the executive branch to reach an objective. They didn't know how to get things done.

But Colson did know, and he quickly established a reputation as the go-to guy for effective problem solving with no questions asked. When a complex plan to turn the old Post Office Department into the semi-independent U.S. Postal Service started to fall apart, it was Colson who tirelessly cut through red tape, massaged bruised egos, managed public relations, and fought numerous turf wars to save it.

Nixon began to notice that assigning a project to Colson produced quick results. When Catholic educators reminded the president of his campaign promise to study parochial schools, Nixon asked for an executive order to be drafted authorizing a commission. But cabinet members and staffers dragged their feet because they questioned the legality of helping a religious organization. Finally in exasperation, the president called Colson into his office on a Friday afternoon and said, "Chuck, I want a commission appointed now. I ordered it a year ago, and no one pays any attention. You do it. Break all the _____ china in this building but have an order for me to sign on my desk Monday morning."

Presidential domestic policy chief John Ehrlichman was out of town for the weekend and Secretary of Health, Education, and Welfare Bob Finch was on vacation. Colson reached Secretary Finch by phone, but neither Ehrlichman nor his assistant returned Colson's calls. Finch authorized the paperwork, Chuck found old executive orders in the files to go by, and everything was on Nixon's desk Monday morning. The president was delighted. Ehrlichman was furious at being circumvented. And Chuck Colson's White House stock rose faster than ever.

After a staff shake-up ahead of the 1970 midterm elections, Colson got more of his assignments directly from Nixon, which H. R. Haldeman saw as a threat to his position as presidential gatekeeper. No one could match Colson's knowledge of the levers of White House power, and no one had his network of contacts outside of government. It was Colson who rallied industry support for the Environmental Protection Agency, staged a one-hundred-thousand-strong march by union members in support of the Vietnam War, and took the lead in damage control after the secret bombing of Cambodia and the killing of four college students by National Guard troops at Kent State in Ohio.

On Monday, June 14, 1971, Chuck Colson attended a White House meeting that would change the course of his life. The day before, the *New York Times* had run a story on page one headlined, "Vietnam Archive: Pentagon Study Traces 3 Decades of Growing U.S. Involvement." Alarmed at first, Colson relaxed when he saw that the account was nothing but a collection of "old memos, position papers, and cables" tracing President Kennedy's first involvement in the Vietnam conflict. In fact, he thought, it might even embarrass the Democrats, who got the country into this mess, and reflect favorably on the Republicans, who were in the process of getting it out.

The next day he changed his mind. According to Colson, the president's national security advisor, Dr. Henry Kissinger, "went into orbit" over the *Times* story. The old memos were part of a confidential forty-seven-volume report, commissioned by Secretary of Defense Robert McNamara, on the history of American involvement in Vietnam from 1945 to 1968. Kissinger agreed that what the *Times* had printed was harmless, but he insisted that whoever knew those things knew other facts that were much more sensitive and possibly damaging to American foreign policy. Worst of all from his perspective, he was deep in the middle of top secret peace talks with the North Vietnamese in Paris. All this self-critical material would set off a new wave of antiwar protest, weakening America's bargaining position.

In a private meeting with Colson, the president flew into a rage, declaring that publishing these Pentagon Papers was a dangerous breach of national security. The courts refused to stop the *Times* from publishing more excerpts, yet America's strongest allies—Great Britain, Australia, Canada—were livid that top secret information involving their governments was being leaked.

The source of these leaks was Daniel Ellsberg, a think-tank analyst who had once worked on Kissinger's staff. If Nixon couldn't keep the

Pentagon Papers out of print, he would do everything he could to discredit Ellsberg. But how? Nixon couldn't legally call in the CIA on a domestic matter like this, and he knew he couldn't bend the FBI's legendary and independent J. Edgar Hoover to his wishes.

Pacing the floor of the Oval Office, President Nixon turned suddenly to Colson and said, "I want him exposed, Chuck. I want the truth about him known. I don't care how you do it, but get it done."

"Yes, sir," Colson replied dutifully. "It will be done."

Step one for Colson was to release a damaging FBI file on Ellsberg to a friendly reporter. The news made hardly a ripple, but information in the file suggested another plan of action. Ellsberg was a psychiatric patient. If Colson couldn't convince the world this burr under the president's saddle was a traitor, then maybe he could imply Ellsberg was a nut case.

A year earlier, a young assistant on Haldeman's staff named Tom Huston chaired a committee set up by the president to see what kind of countermeasures worked best against critical reporters and other people Nixon considered enemies of the administration. The Huston committee concluded that the best tool available was "surreptitious entry"—to steal or photograph sensitive material and/or plant bugging equipment. The only problem was that it was against the law.

The committee report read: "Use of this technique is clearly illegal; it amounts to burglary. It is highly risky and could result in great embarrassment if exposed. However, it is also the most fruitful tool and can produce the type of intelligence which cannot be obtained in any other fashion."

Illegal or not, surreptitious entry was the next step. Haldeman hired a group of men soon known as "the plumbers" because their job was to fix leaks. Presidential staffer Egil "Bud" Krogh was in charge of the team, but it was an ex-FBI agent named George Gordon Liddy who developed a plan to meet the president's objective—stealing the file on Ellsberg's psychiatric treatment. The team needed a quick, quiet five thousand dollars for the job. Without knowing the exact nature of their plan, Chuck Colson secured the money from a political donor.

On September 3, the plumbers broke into the Beverly Hills office of Dr. Lewis Fielding, Daniel Ellsberg's psychiatrist, looking for damaging or embarrassing information about his mental health. Liddy and the plumbers achieved their objective, but the material they found wasn't scandalous enough to have any significant effect on the Pentagon Papers story.

By the fall of 1971, Chuck Colson had a hand in everything around the White House from public relations to seating assignments at presidential state dinners. Nixon admired his endless energy and unquestioning loyalty, as well as the ruthlessness he often used to get the job done. On October 15, *The Wall Street Journal* published a front page feature headlined, "Nixon Hatchet Man: Call It What You Will, Chuck Colson Handles President's Dirty Work." Quoting an ex-aide to the president, the article concluded, "Chuck is a performer. In the process he may break some bones. But the president likes performers."

Inside and outside the White House the "hatchet man" handle stuck. At the time, Colson probably took it as a badge of honor. As the 1972 presidential election season gathered steam, newspapers reported that Colson had once said he would walk over his own grandmother to get Nixon reelected. In a staff memo he made it plain that no sacrifice was too great if it helped achieve their objective: "I am totally unconcerned with anything other than getting the job done. If I bruise feelings or injure anyone's morale, I will be happy to make amends on the morning of November 8 [the day after the election]. . . . Just so you understand me, let me point out the statement in last week's UPI story that I once was reported to have said that 'I would walk over my grandmother if necessary' is absolutely accurate."

Whenever the president was at the White House or at one of his homes in California or Florida, Colson was on twenty-four-hour alert. It was only when the president was on vacation that Colson could reliably expect to sleep through the night without a call from the boss. On Saturday, June 17, 1972, President Nixon was fishing in the Bahamas and Chuck Colson was at home getting ready for a swim in his backyard pool when the phone rang. He heard John Ehrlichman's voice asking, "Where is your friend Howard Hunt these days?" Colson had met Hunt, a former CIA agent, at Brown University alumni gatherings and had recommended him as one of the White House plumbers. Colson hadn't seen or spoken to Hunt in months and had no idea where he was.

Ehrlichman explained that five men had been arrested the night before—breaking into Democratic National Committee headquarters at the Watergate Hotel in Washington. Beginning with a phone number in Howard Hunt's wallet, investigators followed a trail that led to Chuck Colson and the White House. Colson got money for the plumbers when they needed it, but he knew nothing about the Watergate break-in until John Ehrlichman's call.

Though Nixon was reelected that November by one of the largest margins in history—eighteen million votes—and though his press secretary, Ronald Zeigler, characterized the break-in as a "third-rate burglary," the Watergate issue wouldn't go away. The president stridently denied he was involved or that he knew about it in advance, and Colson dutifully believed him.

On Election Day 1972, Chuck wasn't worried yet about Watergate, but he was deeply unsettled about something. The Nixon landslide was an overwhelming endorsement of a president's political agenda on a historic scale. It was the triumph Colson and so many others had given everything to achieve. And yet that night, as he later described so vividly in his book *Born Again*, Colson felt not exhilaration but emptiness:

My insides were as deadened as the air in the room and the slow beat of the music. My lack of exhilaration made no sense. Being part of electing a president was the fondest ambition of my life. For three long years I had committed everything I had, every ounce of energy to Richard Nixon's cause. Nothing else had mattered. We had no time together as a family, no social life, no vacations. So why could my tongue not taste the flavor of this hour of conquest?

The drumbeat of Watergate grew louder. On February 7, 1973, the Senate unanimously voted to empanel a special committee, chaired by Senator Sam Ervin of North Carolina, to investigate the break-in. Chuck believed the best way for the president to deal with the controversy was to root out whoever was responsible and do all he could to assist the investigators. During his last official meeting as a presidential advisor, on February 13, Colson was recorded by a secret White House taping system as he advised his commander-in-chief: "Whoever did order Watergate, let it out! Get rid of it now, take our losses!" The president, Chuck later wrote, "seemed almost paralyzed by Watergate, unable or unwilling to face harsh realities."

Colson resigned his White House position as planned and returned to his law practice in March 1973. Conflict of interest rules had kept him from maintaining ties with former clients while he was in government service. One of the first orders of business, then, was to reestablish relationships with union and corporate chiefs he had worked with before. Among those men was Tom Phillips, chairman of Raytheon Corporation, a major defense contractor and the largest employer in New England.

Chuck scheduled a round of appointments with several Raytheon decision-makers including his friend Brainerd Holmes, former head of the government's manned spacecraft program and now a Raytheon executive vice president. Later in the day, Tom Phillips sent word that he'd like to see Chuck too before he left. As Colson headed for Phillips's office, Holmes stopped him to warn him that Phillips had undergone "quite a change—some kind of religious experience. I don't really understand it, but it's quite important to him."

Chuck could scarcely imagine someone as hard driving and aggressive as Tom Phillips going off on any kind of religious jag. But when he walked into Tom's office he immediately sensed there was something different about him. He seemed more relaxed and self-assured than ever before. He acted not only happy but deeply fulfilled in a way Chuck seldom, if ever, saw among his professional colleagues. Most executive officers of major corporations carried a load of worries; the focus was on performance and success at any cost. Tom, by contrast, projected a serenity both mysterious and appealing. Chuck noticed "a new compassion in his eyes and a gentleness in his voice." Furthermore, Raytheon's profits were at an all-time high.

Chuck was intrigued. Finally he ventured, "Brainerd tells me that you have become very involved in some religious activities."

"Yes, that's true, Chuck," Phillips answered. "I have accepted Jesus Christ. I have committed my life to Him, and it has been the most marvelous experience of my whole life."

Completely floored and not knowing what to say, Colson made a strategic retreat: "Uh, maybe sometime you and I can discuss that, Tom." Of all the reasons his friend could have given for his new outlook on life, that was the last one Chuck had imagined. Later he would learn that Tom had happened upon a Billy Graham crusade one night in New York. Curious and with nothing better to do, he slipped into Madison Square Garden to have a look. Listening to Graham's message, Tom felt an unfamiliar sense that he needed Christ in his life and an unexplainable assurance that He was with him. Metaphysical and internal as it was, it was hard to articulate the change he felt; describing it was anticlimactic. But the experience was absolutely real, the transformation permanent.

Tom's story struck a chord with Chuck. A sense of emptiness and lack of direction had been building up inside him for a long time. He'd noticed it particularly since the night of President Nixon's reelection. Through the second inaugural and his last few months in the White

House, that emptiness had persisted where there should have been the contented afterglow of hard-won success. Back at his law firm, he threw himself into his old role as senior partner and strategic leader. He was rich and successful and only forty-one. But something wasn't right. He felt himself distracted and drifting in meetings. That had never happened to him in his life.

What was missing? Why did his life feel so empty and pointless? He didn't know. He thought about it every day and many nights. Maybe Tom Phillips had discovered whatever it was Colson himself was looking for.

[CHAPTER 3]
A Vision in the Mirror

M eanwhile in Washington, cracks appeared in the president's Watergate story. Rumors flew that White House insiders knew ahead of time about the break-in and were trying to cover up their involvement. On April 13, 1973, Colson agreed to meet with John Ehrlichman once more to advise him and the presidential team. Again Chuck stuck to his earlier recommendation.

"I am convinced," he said in a conversation recorded by the secret White House taping system, "that either the grand jury or the Ervin hearings will expose any 'higher-ups' who had foreknowledge in involvement in the Watergate. . . . If those who did in fact have knowledge of the Watergate or who were in any other way involved in the Watergate, are now exposed, there is a chance at least to avoid the Ervin hearings and to terminate the grand jury. . . . My recommendation therefore is that those involved in authorizing, planning, or approving the Watergate operation either come forward or be exposed now. To wait only incites more serious charges."

Some commentators put the blame squarely on Colson. The April thirty *Washington Post* headline reported, "Aides Say Colson Approved

Bugging." Colson's rebuttal was at the bottom of column four. But Howard Hunt himself had said Colson had nothing to do with Watergate, and other testimony proved Colson was never present at any of the secret White House strategy sessions involving the plumbers. To his relief, Chuck learned that he wasn't a grand jury target. On August 7, the Ervin committee took a recess and Chuck Colson and his wife took a vacation to Maine.

Stopping to visit Chuck's parents on their way north, he and Patty were only a few miles from Tom Phillips's house in the Boston suburbs. Colson felt an urge to see his friend that he couldn't explain. When Chuck called Tom to ask if he could drop by, Tom welcomed the visit. That Sunday night, August 12, Chuck went alone to Tom's, and the two men walked out onto the screened porch to talk.

The conversation turned to the changes in Tom's life Chuck had noticed. Tom, who had never shared his Christian testimony with any-one before, explained that in spite of his business success he had felt "a terrible emptiness" in his life. After he'd looked everywhere else, he looked in the Bible. "Something made me realize I needed a personal relationship with God," he explained, "forced me to search." After Tom listened to Billy Graham that night in New York, all the pieces had fallen into place.

The two talked late into the evening, with Colson detailing the Watergate accusations against him and describing the vicious nature of national politics. Tom replied, "If you had put your faith in God, and if your cause were just, He would have guided you." As he spoke he picked up a paperback copy of *Mere Christianity*. Its author, C. S. Lewis, who died in 1963, was a distinguished professor at Oxford and Cambridge and a prolific layman whose writings on Christianity appealed especially to readers interested in the intellectual underpinnings of the faith.

"I don't think you'll understand what I'm saying about God until you're willing to face yourself honestly and squarely." He held up the book. "This is the first step."

He read aloud from the chapter on pride, which Lewis called "the greatest sin."

Pride leads to every other vice: it is the complete anti-God state of mind. . . . As long as you are proud you cannot know God. A proud man is always looking down on things and people. And, of course, as long as you are looking down, you cannot see something that is above you. For Pride is spiritual cancer: it eats up the very possibility of love, or contentment, or even common sense.

The words struck Colson like a thunderbolt—Lewis's condemnation was for him; Christ's admonition was for him; Jesus's sacrifice was for him. Spiritual fulfillment was what had been missing from his life. But he had seen too many bogus foxhole conversions in the Marine Corps to believe he could make so enormous a change all at once. He wanted to think about it. Tom loaned him the book and also jotted down the name of Doug Coe, a friend in Washington who organized prayer breakfasts and other gatherings for Christian fellowship.

Driving back to his parents' house Chuck was soon crying so hard he had to pull over. That night, Charles Colson was transformed from within. What no outside experience could do, what no financial or professional success could produce, a spiritual force from the inside accomplished in an instant. Nixon's hatchet man became the servant of the Lord. He wasn't sure how, but he would redirect all the intellect and energy that brought him business and political success to serving Christ. He affirmed his decision with Patty during their Maine vacation.

History would later muddle two important facts in the story of Chuck Colson. One of them is that contrary to popular myth, Colson did not experience any sort of jailhouse conversion. He became a Christian before he had any idea he might go to prison. What is true is that Colson didn't say anything public about his new spiritual life. He thought it was nobody's business but his and God's. His wife, Patty, a lifelong Catholic, scarcely knew what to think of her newly evangelical husband. The few confidants who knew what happened, including his friend and partner David Shapiro (who was Jewish), also wondered how this hard-driving, win-at-all-cost character could change so abruptly.

Near the end of his week in Maine, Chuck wrote to Tom Phillips telling him he'd thought through his new perspective on faith and had dedicated himself fully to Christ. Tom celebrated Chuck's decision in a phone call, and encouraged him to connect with Doug Coe when he returned to Washington. During Colson's first week back at work, Doug appeared unannounced at his office to say Tom had read him Chuck's letter.

"This is just great, just great," he enthused, taking a seat and throwing a leg over the arm of his chair. Surprised and a little put out at first with Coe's familiar manner, Colson quickly came to appreciate his sincerity and his eagerness to encourage other Christians.

Tom Phillips and Doug Coe were the first two in a long and continuing line of figures whose lives, careers, and Christian walks made them essential threads in the tapestry of Prison Fellowship Ministries. Years before PF was established, and even before Chuck Colson had the faintest notion of the personal legal battles that lay ahead, a core group of men began to coalesce around him who would guide, encourage, hold accountable, and exhort him for the next thirty years. Some were his polar opposites on policy issues; some were younger and others older; and one distinguished legislator had already done jail time. Doug Coe soon organized a small but intensely faithful group of Washington heavyweights that later nurtured Colson's spiritual growth, supported him through the darkest days of Watergate and imprisonment, laid the foundation for Prison Fellowship, and played essential roles in launching and developing the ministry.

Within days of their first meeting, Coe introduced Colson to Senator Harold Hughes of Iowa, previously governor of the state, one-time truck driver, reformed alcoholic, former prisoner, and one of the Nixon administration's most outspoken critics. Though they were worlds apart politically, Hughes welcomed Colson warmly as a new friend in Christ. Through Coe, Colson also met Minnesota congressman (later governor) Al Quie, and former Texas congressman Graham Purcell. God was providentially bringing the right circle of Christian support to Chuck.

On December 6, 1973, Colson attended for the first time a regular biweekly prayer breakfast in a White House VIP dining room. Some of the others there that morning had been his political enemies for years; some he had blasted in the press. But now all of them—Catholic, Protestant, and Jew—celebrated their common bond as children of God.

CBS White House correspondent Dan Rather spied Colson entering the presidential compound. At the daily press briefing later in the morning, he asked the assistant press secretary what Colson was doing at the White House. Watergate hearings had escalated and were saturating the newswires. As former special counsel to the president, and as one connected to the Watergate burglars by that mysterious phone number in Howard Hunt's wallet, Colson was a target of interest for the media. He had supposedly long since severed his official ties with Nixon, and here he was pulling up to the White House.

After hemming and hawing a little, the press official told Rather and the rest of the press corps that Colson had come for the biweekly prayer breakfast.

Prayer breakfast? Nixon's hatchet man? That sent the gaggle of reporters flying to the telephones to report the headline of the day: "Colson's found religion!" Many commentators questioned his sincerity or derided the whole thing as a sham. Now that he was in trouble because of Watergate, Colson was hiding behind some religious façade. When the first calls reached Colson's law office asking for a comment, he was furious and defensive. He insisted that his faith was not a matter for public discussion.

The Watergate inquiry dragged on into 1974. Though Colson had been assured he wasn't a target of the investigation, he was eventually indicted on three Watergate counts. All three were soon dismissed. But there was also an indictment against him stemming from the earlier Pentagon Papers burglary—stealing Ellsberg's treatment file from his psychiatrist's office—by the same team of plumbers.

As the case against him moved forward, Colson faced several options. One was to plead innocent to the Ellsberg charges and go to trial. Another was to accept a deal from the prosecutors to plead guilty in exchange for a suspended sentence. The plea bargain was tempting, but the truth was Chuck hadn't committed that crime. What he had done wrong—publicly undermining Ellsberg's credibility in the same way so many reporters and Watergate suspects had tried to undermine his own—was something he hadn't been charged with. He had known nothing specific about the break-in at Dr. Fielding's. But in his conscience he was convinced that he had wronged Ellsberg by distorting the truth while Ellsberg was under investigation.

After a series of emotional prayer sessions with his new circle of Christian friends, Chuck believed the right thing to do in God's eyes was pass up the plea bargain and plead guilty to a crime he was never accused of: influencing the "due administration of justice" by use of a "threatening letter or communication." Both his lawyer and the judge were astonished; they'd never heard of the law Colson claimed he had broken. Here's the second great misconception about Colson and Watergate. He was not imprisoned for any crime directly connected to the Watergate break-in, but for violating Daniel Ellsberg's right to a fair trial, a crime he brought to the court's attention himself.

Colson explained years later that he pled guilty to protect innocent junior staffers whose careers would have been ruined by false accusations against them, and also to protect his Christian witness. As long as the question of guilt hung over him, he knew he could never be an effective spokesman for his newfound faith. He didn't become a Christian when he went to prison; he went to prison because he had become a Christian.

Colson had no idea he would actually be incarcerated. A number of people tried on Watergate-related offenses had avoided time behind bars, and Colson figured that because of the relatively light sentencing guidelines for his crime, he would go free as well. His one-to-three-year prison term was a blast of cold water in the face—unexpected, shocking, terrifying.

Sent first to a minimum-security prison in Maryland, Colson later went to a federal prison on the grounds of Maxwell Air Force Base in Alabama. Living there in an open dormitory with fifty other men, some of them violent criminals and murderers, Colson saw a life he had never imagined that appalled him. Prison did more than punish the men incarcerated, it dehumanized them. It broke their spirits. It offered no chance to make restitution. It severed their connections with the outside world and things that were good.

Arriving at Maxwell in September 1974, Colson had to strip naked and put on prison underwear and a uniform. He got a new identity, Prisoner 23226, and a new address, Dormitory G. Looking around the courtyard, his first impression was that the inmates seemed so listless. They drifted without purpose, staring ahead expressionless. The yard was eerily quiet; there was no conversation. When he opened the door to Dormitory G, Colson almost gagged at the stench of stale bodies and tobacco smoke. Paint peeled from the grimy yellow walls. One overworked ceiling fan stirred the rancid atmosphere and swirled up wisps of dust from the filthy floors and windowsills.

Colson's dorm mates included a former official with the American Medical Association, moonshiners, drug dealers, military veterans, and petty thugs. Maxwell wasn't a maximum security prison, so the prisoners were supposedly not prone to deadly violence. But they had cliques based on race and gang memberships that were hostile to each other. Longtime prisoners learned how to maintain control through physical and verbal threats and intimidation. They weren't afraid to fight.

One widely feared black inmate walked up to Colson while he was mopping the floor and asked, "How do you like living with the scum after having servants waiting on you in the White House?"

Colson paused for a beat, then answered, "I was mopping floors before you were born, and I was in the Marine Corps when you were in diapers." That earned Chuck the prisoner's respect, and the respect of the clique that followed him.

Colson began a diary of his prison experience. "If the purpose of prison was rehabilitation," he wrote, "it was a miserable failure." His fellow inmates generally came from broken and disturbed families, and measured success by altogether different standards than on the outside. In prison, violence made you a hero. The meaner you were, the better. Any sign of vulnerability could get you killed. You didn't help others, but you took advantage of them. All the usual standards of civilized life were turned topsy-turvy.

Criminals came into prison angry, poorly educated, with poor job skills, most of them with life-threatening drug addictions, no money, and no emotional support system. When they came out, if anything, they were worse. They made connections with other criminals, learned new crime techniques, hardened in their own drug use and experimented with others. They were more than ever the scum of society, the outcast, and the unwanted.

Chuck concluded that prison programs paid lip service to inmates' needs on the surface, but did nothing to address the fundamental problems. Most of all, he saw how spiritually empty the offenders' lives were. This, he believed, was the wellspring of every other problem. If prisoners could be spiritually restored, they would drive improvements in other areas of their own lives. When he became a Christian, Chuck saw all the sin and shortfalls in his life clearly for the first time. He was convinced that by becoming Christians, inmates would at last look honestly at themselves, see the sin in their lives, and change from the inside out.

In a letter to his Christian brothers in Washington, Chuck described the insights the Bible had given him about why his life had taken so dramatic a turn:

> In Hebrews 2, there is an eloquent statement of why God became mortal in the person and flesh of Christ so that He could experience the pain and suffering and feelings of other humans. He had to become one of them to truly love them and lead them to redemption. There is an analogy. No one can observe what it is like to be a prisoner. Most of them are not treated like human beings; there is the slow erosion of their souls. I doubt that any visitor could feel it—but I now can. I know the indignities and frustrations, the sense of loneliness and isolation, the loss of individual pride and self-respect, the cumulative impact of a series of little and big things that are familiar to a prison. I have also felt the terrible spiritual longing of so many of these unfortunate souls. I know now that the Lord has a plan for me and that this experience will enable me to minister in a way I never could have otherwise—and a way that perhaps few others could. It wouldn't have been what I would have chosen—but then what I would choose is not what this is about.

He found out later that his Washington prayer group had read Hebrews 2 the same day.

Though Chuck studied his Bible faithfully and readily professed his Christianity, he hesitated to start a formal Bible study in prison because he didn't want prisoners and staff to think he was angling for some kind of control. But so many prisoners came to him for advice and asked him questions about Scripture that he finally began leading a study. They sensed the peace he felt even in so hostile a place and wanted to know where he found it. Colson modeled the sessions after the ones he shared with Doug, Al, Graham, and Harold. Openly embracing Christianity behind bars usually invited taunts and threats—other inmates saw it as a sign of weakness. But these faithful worshipers quietly persevered. The feeling of peace they radiated attracted more men to their circle, and still more came when a dangerously sick prisoner inexplicably recovered after the group held a prayer vigil at his bedside.

On January 31, 1975, Chuck Colson was released from prison by a judge citing his family difficulties. Colson's father had died while he was incarcerated, and his son Christian was arrested on drug charges. Other than his family and the crowd of reporters on his lawn, the first person he and Patty saw when they walked in the door that night was Doug Coe. Doug and his family had put fresh flowers throughout the house, set out snacks, and built a roaring fire in the Colson fireplace.

During his first months of freedom Chuck thought hard about how he should spend the rest of his life. He could try to rebuild his law practice, which Patty enthusiastically supported. Another option was to serve on the boards of companies looking for influence on Capitol Hill, or to be a consultant for them. Felon or not, he had the ear of important people in the capital. He could likely make millions using his influence to spin policies and legislation in ways favorable to his clients.

There was also the prospect of some sort of prison ministry. He resisted it at first, but the idea kept coming back to him. He remembered a conversation in prison with Archie, an imposing black inmate whose arms were covered with tattoos.

"Hey, Colson," Archie had said, "what are you going to do for us when you get out?"

"I'm going to help you somehow," Colson replied. "I'll never forget this stinking place or you guys."

"That's what you all say," Archie snapped. "You big shots come and go and always forget about us. Ain't nobody who cares about us. Nobody."

"I'll remember, Archie."

"Bull——!" Archie answered, his eyes glowing with scorn as he walked away.

In the months after his release, some friends and family encouraged Chuck to apply to have his law license reinstated while others nudged him toward the corporate world. His old boss Richard Nixon advised, "You can do big things in business. Remember, you aren't beaten. You have tremendous abilities. I know it. Go out now and make some money for your family."

Whether or not a business career was in his future, Chuck knew, as he later wrote in his book *Life Sentence*, that he wasn't cut out for prison ministry.

> Though I often anguished for the men I'd left behind in prison and was angered over the injustices to which they were subjected, prison work was not for me. Several friends had suggested that I develop some kind of ministry to inmates. But the thought of going back into prison chilled me; the stench was still pungent in my nostrils. Maybe I could give a few talks about prison reform, perhaps prod friends still in politics into doing something. But it was not my career.

An experience one Saturday morning completely transformed his thinking. Standing in front of the shaving mirror, he saw a series of pictures flashing across his mind:

> Men in prison gray moving about. Classes. Discussion. Prayers.
>
> "Of course, of course," I whispered as if in response to obvious commands. "Take the prisoners out, teach them, return them to prisons to build Christian fellowships. Spread these fellowships through every penitentiary in America."
>
> I was now wide awake, my heart racing, every nerve in my body alert and exhilarated. . . . Before my eyes was a simple plan with every detail fitting into place. . . . I saw sharply focused pictures—of smiling men and women, streaming out of prisons, of Bibles and study groups, of fellowship around tables. Then I realized something else: I had never thought of anything like this before. It was not my idea, but something I was reacting to.

These mental images lasted but a few seconds, then they were gone. I had never experienced anything like this before or since.

Was it of God? Or just a flash inspiration, like any good idea which pops suddenly unto one's consciousness? Even as I splashed cold water on my face, I felt an unusual assurance.

Chuck immediately called Harold Hughes, who suggested they meet with Senator James Eastland, the Mississippi Democrat who chaired the Judiciary Committee, which oversaw the American prison system. Cordial and encouraging though he was during their two-hour meeting, Eastland had never been inside a prison and failed to follow up on his promise to look into how he might help turn Colson's vision into action.

Reaching a dead end with Senator Eastland, Colson and Hughes met with Norman Carlson, director of the Bureau of Prisons. In Carlson's office they explained that they wanted to furlough prisoners, equip them as Bible teachers, then send them back to teach other inmates.

Miraculously, Carlson agreed to let them try. At least part of the reason was an experience Carlson and his wife had at Terminal Island Prison in Southern California. "On Sunday we went to chapel," Carlson remembered. "During the service the chaplain asked for spontaneous prayers. An inmate in the back prayed for my wife and me. I was surprised that he did that."

"He's a Christian," Chuck answered. "We're taught to pray for those in authority. I did it for the warden at Maxwell."

"I know that, but I'm the one keeping him in prison."

"That man prayed for you because he loved you."

Colson and the others set up a modest operation under the umbrella of the Fellowship Foundation, which had been founded by Doug Coe. Arriving in Washington as a staffer with Oregon Senator Mark Hatfield, Coe had established the Fellowship Foundation to give national and world leaders of every political stripe a forum for communication and spiritual renewal according to the teachings of Christ. Its high-profile event every year was the National Prayer Breakfast. Far more important was Fellowship House, an elegant Washington home that was once the Danish embassy, where powerful public figures could meet, talk, and pray out of the public spotlight, any time of the day or night.

The plan was to bring twelve carefully selected inmates to Washington on two-week furloughs, teach them to lead in-prison Bible studies, and then return them to their facilities to put those lessons into practice. They would live in the basement of the Good News Mission, a halfway house, but then have their classes and social events at Fellowship House twenty minutes away. When neighbors around Fellowship House saw a newspaper article about the project, they panicked. Fearing a drop in property values and a rise in crime, they hired a high-profile lawyer and threatened to sue.

Doug Coe began meeting with skittish property owners to assure them everything would be all right. The first group of prisoners arrived in Washington on November 2, 1975. A week went by without any of the neighbors taking them to court. Then came what Colson called "a crucial event." Fellowship House regularly hosted luncheons for Bible studies and other groups. They invited the neighbors to a lunch that week where the visiting inmates, dressed in street clothes, were scattered among the tables with other guests. When Chuck invited some of the locals to try and pick out the prisoners, nine out of ten identified the wrong people. Soon neighbors and prisoners began mingling and talking freely, and that was the end of the complaints.

Chuck and his colleagues scheduled other seminars, refining the curriculum as they went. Still uncertain about his long-range plans, Colson prepared for the publication of *Born Again*, the story of his career and spiritual journey. The book, released February 18, 1976, was an instant best seller. The entire first printing of forty thousand was sold out before the title hit the shelves.

After a grueling yet exhilarating international tour as an author,

Chuck spent a quiet few days with Patty on the Oregon coast in a house owned by Senator Hatfield. In the same way he had pondered his Christian commitment on the Maine coast the year before, he was now considering how he should live out that commitment.

Patty sensed his searching, and they talked as they had many times before about what God would have them do. Reversing his earlier position, Chuck now felt sure that he should dedicate himself to prison ministry, but he sensed Patty's hesitation. That night she admitted to him that as good as their marriage had always been, with Christ in the forefront it had been better than ever. If Christ was calling him into the prisons, she declared, "I'm with you all the way."

Two days later, he and Fred Rhodes, a strong Christian friend and prison ministry advocate, and former chairman of the Postal Rate Commission, began preparing incorporation papers. On August 9, 1976, Prison Fellowship Ministries officially opened for business in a three-room office in Arlington, Virginia, with one good typewriter, one bad typewriter, and a few desks made out of surplus doors.

The young ministry faced long odds in setting out to reform America's prison system. It was a case of David, faithful but hopelessly small and inexperienced, against a Goliath of bureaucracy, inertia, turf wars, power, politics, and unpromising history.

[CHAPTER 4]

Desperate Legacy

Though there have been criminals as long as there have been laws, the idea of imprisonment as punishment is relatively recent. Penitentiaries were unknown in America before the Revolutionary War. The few jails and prisons in the Colonies held mostly debtors or suspects awaiting judgment. Magistrates typically punished local citizens guilty of petty crimes according to their social station. Higher-ups paid a fine, while lower class offenders spent a few hours in the stocks. In Massachusetts Colony, for example, convicted drunks either paid five shillings into the public coffers or sat three hours in the public stocks. Strangers guilty of similar offenses were generally whipped and banished from the community.

According to *The Oxford History of the Prison*, the primary goal of the judicial system was deterrence: "Magistrates in colonial America never considered the possibility of rehabilitation through punishment. The aim was not to reform the offender but to frighten him into lawful behavior."

If a monetary fine, public humiliation, or corporal punishment failed to correct the offender's deportment, he was generally executed by hanging. Even relatively minor crimes, such as theft, were punishable by death on the third offense. From the perspective of America's Puritan settlers, crime was a reflection of the sinful nature of man; it was ever present and unavoidable. The remedies then were either to scare a criminal into controlling his sinful tendencies, to run him out of town to keep those tendencies from threatening others, or, failing all else, to end his sinful life. In colonial New York, about 20 percent of all offenses were punishable by death, including pickpocketing, horse stealing, and burglary.

In 1787, the Philadelphia Society for Alleviating the Miseries of Public Prisons, championed by the prominent physician and signer of the Declaration of Independence, Dr. Benjamin Rush, petitioned the Pennsylvania legislature to institute solitary confinement as an alternative to execution. Their novel idea was to use imprisonment to change people's behavior. They proposed isolating lawbreakers to compel them to focus on their actions, ponder their sin, repent, and redirect their lives in a good and godly direction. Wrongdoers should not be whipped or humiliated, but encouraged to change.

They based their model of prison management, which came to be called the Pennsylvania System, on five principles: 1) prisoners should not be treated with malice; individual suffering, not institutional abuse, would be more effective in changing their behavior; 2) solitary confinement could prevent further corruption among prisoners; 3) solitary confinement could achieve penitence and repentance of the offender; 4) solitary confinement was true punishment since people are social beings; 5) solitary confinement was cost effective because isolation would rehabilitate prisoners sooner and require fewer guards.

The legislature authorized the remodeling of part of the Walnut Street Jail in Philadelphia into a "penitentiary" where convicts, living alone in their cells, could practice penitence and seek forgiveness. Opened in 1790, it was the template for prisons in other states throughout the new Republic. Thomas Eddy, a wealthy Quaker businessman and prison reformer from New York, spearheaded construction of a similar new penitentiary in Greenwich Village. When finished in 1799 it cost the state government more than two hundred thousand dollars—more than it spent during the same period on roads, schools, or the state militia.

Eddy believed prisoners could be reformed and that the main objective of imprisonment should be to address the "evil passions and corrupt habits which are the sources of guilt." He promoted "regular labor and exact temperance." Beginning with one inmate trained as a cobbler, Eddy set up a factory making shoes and boots, with the cobbler teaching several inmates who then passed along the skill to others. A visitor noted that while prisoners with no work to do looked "melancholy," the sixty or so journeymen cobblers seemed "approaching to cheerfulness." Useful work under humane circumstances clearly improved prisoners' attitudes and behavior.

Eddy set up a prison chapel and invited local clergy to preach there. He also started a night school to teach reading, writing, and arithmetic. Another innovation was a system of incentives that awarded model inmates visiting time with their families and gave them cash payments for prison labor upon their release.

Eddy was frustrated that some ex-offenders committed new crimes and returned to prison. One of the most famous was Charlotte Thomas, arrested and imprisoned five times over sixteen years for larceny. Eddy also faced prison uprisings and escapes. Inmates sometimes took jail keepers as hostages. When that happened, musket fire and occasional military intervention restored order.

These early Pennsylvania and New York reformers learned lessons that later generations would lose, rediscover, and refine time and again over the next two hundred years. They believed individual sin was the source of crime and that reflection and repentance were the only true cures. They observed that prisoners who worked were more content than those who sat listlessly all day with nothing to do. They saw an advantage in teaching prisoners to read and write, and in a system of rewards for good behavior.

They also recognized an inevitable connection between prisons and politics. Prisons required government money and generated government jobs, which made them important political plums. Thomas Eddy was a rare man of independent means and no political aspirations who worked for prison reform simply because he wanted to serve the public good and benefit offenders.

Yet he was still vulnerable to the political winds. The elections of 1800 drove out many officeholders sympathetic to New York Quakers, so that Eddy's popularity with the public bureaucrats took a sharp downward turn. Prison conditions declined, and Eddy took much of the blame even though the problems weren't his fault. In 1797 there had been 123 inmates at the New York prison. Six years later, there were nearly 400 in the same building and no money for new construction. When Eddy was away on business in 1803, three prisoners and an innocent bystander died during an escape attempt. Hounded by newly appointed prison inspectors under the hostile political regime, Eddy resigned his seat on the prison board.

Only thirteen years after the first purpose-built penitentiary in America opened its doors, the prison system was already overcrowded and underfunded. Even the groundbreaking Walnut Street Penitentiary in Philadelphia was so overcrowded by 1801 that its director quit in disgust. Without altruistic visionaries like Eddy to enlighten and inspire them, opportunistic politicians shifted their attention from the prisoners to the political clout prisons gave them.

New York's second prison, in the town of Auburn, was run by Elam Lynds, a captain during the Revolutionary War whose imposing military bearing was accented by a livid scar across his left cheek, from the outside corner of his eye to the corner of his mouth. Captain Lynds's philosophy of prison management was completely opposite from what Eddy's had been, and the state legislature soon gave him the means to impose far stricter punishment. In 1819, two years after the first prisoners arrived at Auburn, a new state penal code allowed prison officials to punish rule breakers with bread and water and solitary confinement as before, but also with irons, stocks, and up to thirty-nine lashes. Lynds issued each prison keeper a cat-o'-nine-tails or "cat," a braided whip with multiple ends that made several welts with each stroke.

At first, keepers resisted using the cat. In one incident, Lynds ordered three prisoners whipped. The keeper refused, and Lynds fired him on the spot. A second keeper refused and was fired, and then a third. A blacksmith working nearby volunteered to do the whipping. After he finished and left the prison, his neighbors intercepted him in the street, stripped off his clothes, covered him with hot tar and feathers, and carried him around the prison walls on a rail. But applying the cat was soon commonplace.

Auburn divided its prisoners into three classes: hardened offenders, the less dangerous, and the least guilty and depraved. The first group lived in complete isolation day and night in cells seven feet long, seven feet high, and three and a half feet wide. Others worked in groups during the day and lived in solitary confinement at night.

Isolated and forced to maintain absolute silence, prisoners suffered horribly. In *With Liberty for Some*, Scott Christianson wrote,

> According to the prison physician, their "sedentary life in the prison, as it calls into aid the debilitating passions of melancholy, grief, etc., rapidly hastens the progress of pulmonary disease." Several [prisoners] had apparently gone insane. When one convict's door was opened, he sprang out and leaped from the fourth-floor gallery onto the stone pavement. Another was discovered to have bashed his head against the cell wall until he had destroyed one of his eyes. Another had slashed his veins with a piece of tin and bled to death. Governor Joseph C. Yates personally visited the prison and was so horrified by what he saw that he pardoned some survivors on the spot.

And yet the state legislature believed in more security and more discipline. They abolished communal cells at Thomas Eddy's old prison in Greenwich Village and put all state prisoners in solitary confinement at night. They instituted strict military-style discipline, with each prisoner being issued a uniform and an identity number to use instead of a name. The prisoners marched in lockstep from place to place, were banned from speaking at any time day or night, assigned a prison job, and were subject to relentless and never-varying schedules for work, sleep, and meals. Keepers wearing moccasins spied on prisoners from hidden walkways to make sure they never talked.

The keepers could whip prisoners for almost any infraction real or imagined. It was illegal for a guard to whip anyone without a higher official present, though this rule was most often honored in the breach as the sad story of a young prisoner named Rachel Welch so vividly shows. An Irish immigrant imprisoned shortly after her arrival in America, Welch was sentenced to three months in solitary confinement for breaking prison rules. During this time, she conceived a child by the prison cook who brought her meals. She died in prison days after giving birth.

An autopsy showed she had not only been whipped in violation of the state law against flogging women prisoners, but she had been whipped while pregnant. A prison keeper named Ebenezer Cobb had beaten her because she complained she was pregnant and threw a bowl of mush at him. His flogging ruptured her uterus. Two black male inmates who held her down for him couldn't testify, since as prisoners their testimony was not admissible in court.

Cobb was convicted of assault and battery, fined twenty-five dollars, and allowed to stay on the job. Neither Lynds nor any other official was prosecuted. "As a result," Christianson reported, "the use and intensity of flogging drastically increased." Though state inspectors later described the women's quarters at Auburn as "a specimen of the most disgusting and appalling features of the old system of prison management at the worst period of its history," it was 1893 before the state funded a separate prison for women, sixty-seven years after Rachel Welch died.

Through the middle years of the nineteenth century, American prison officials and politicians seemed to lose any interest in reforming inmates. The prison population was generally cruelly treated, poorly clothed and fed, and often forced to work for contractors or private operators who paid a fee to the state. The driving force behind prison policies became neither reforming the offender nor protecting society, but making a profit. The private operators at Sing Sing prison in New York used prison labor to run a marble quarry, a blacksmith shop, a brass foundry, hat-making and carpentry shops, and other enterprises. Inmates were beaten mercilessly if they failed to finish a day's assigned work, and they suffered hunger and even starvation. Individual cells were smaller than at Auburn, only six and a half feet high and three feet, three inches across.

Visiting Eastern Penitentiary near Philadelphia in 1842, the famous English novelist Charles Dickens saw offenders in isolation driven insane by their punishment. Dickens pronounced solitary confinement "cruel and wrong," adding that "this slow and daily tampering with the mysteries of the brain [are] immeasurably worse than any torture of the body."

It was 1870 before prison operators formally revisited the idea of using incarceration to rehabilitate offenders as Benjamin Rush and Thomas Eddy had originally proposed. That year Dr. Enoch Cobb Wines, a reform-minded member of the New York Prison Association, organized the National Prison Congress in Cincinnati. The Congress passed a Declaration of Principles stating that the "supreme aim of prison discipline is the reformation of criminals, not the infliction of vindictive suffering." The declaration promoted sanitary conditions, rewards for good conduct, education, and the idea that "moral forces" were better at reforming prisoners than physical or psychological punishment.

A reformatory at Elmira, New York, opened in 1876 to put the

National Prison Congress principles into practice on young first-time offenders. Its warden, Zebulon R. Brockaway, set up an ambitious program of merits and demerits, job training, and even the first inmate newspaper, *The Summary*. After a few years Brockaway concluded that modern criminals were

> to a considerable extent the product of our civilization and also of emigration to our shore from the degenerated populations of crowded European marts. . . . Until the source of supply is stanched, there is no safety for society but in quarantining and curing . . . the criminally infected individuals brought to our attention by their crimes.

Xenophobic and racist as he is to modern ears, Brockaway made some tantalizing observations. One was that when it comes to criminal behavior, thoughts precede actions. Brockaway believed that individual "mental powers"—innermost emotional and spiritual currents—determined more than anything else what someone would do. Another observation he made was that prison can be more than just a holding pen; it can treat and help cure the "criminally infected."

Most prison boards simply ignored the National Prison Congress recommendations, continuing their practices of corporal punishment, torture, and hiring out inmates—a practice ripe for graft and embezzlement as well as mistreatment of offenders. Prisons in Florida infamously flogged inmates to death or hung them by their thumbs until they died; New Jersey prisoners were doused with alcohol and set on fire; in Ohio inmates sat naked in puddles of water and received electric shocks. One offender released from a Missouri penitentiary, where rule breakers were whipped and the wounds sponged with salt water, declared he took "a diabolical delight in holding up trains and dynamiting the express safe. I was a real, hard-boiled outlaw and proud of it because I felt that anything I did was mild compared with the wrongs that society was inflicting on the men in its prisons."

American prisons carried this legacy of prisoner abuse into the twentieth century, where in addition to everything else, offenders became the involuntary subjects of various medical and psychological experiments. Some of the most notorious involved the pseudoscience of eugenics, the practice of "improving" the human race by encouraging "superior" men and women to have children and discouraging or preventing "inferior" people from procreating. Former slaves, immigrants, Native Americans, and other "inferior" races were prime suspects in the "decline" of humanity, along with the "insane, feeble-minded, and wayward." Princeton psychologist Henry H. Goddard deduced that about 89 percent of criminals were mentally defective and that "every feeble-minded person is a potential criminal."

Others disagreed. Frederick H. Wines, whose father Enoch led the first National Prison Congress, strongly and categorically opposed any connection between criminal behavior and physical characteristics, declaring it took no measurements or list of physical traits "to enable a common man, familiar with criminals through his relation to them as an officer of the police or of a court or prison, to describe their most obvious and striking characteristics."

After a stint in jail himself, a labor leader reported, "I have heard people refer to the 'criminal countenance.' I never saw one. Any man or woman looks like a criminal behind bars." British physician Dr. Charles Goring reported that his study of three thousand prisoners, all of whom had been sentenced at least twice, showed no noteworthy differences between them and a control group of Oxford undergraduates.

The first significant wave of change in American corrections came not as a result of religion or science or politics, but through the courts. From the colonial period to the 1940s, judges had little to say about prisons and prisoners. Almost no cases came before them because with rare exceptions prisoners weren't allowed to write letters and couldn't afford lawyers. Judges and clerks routinely ignored the few petitions that did get through to them.

The door to reform by way of the judiciary opened a crack in 1941 when the Supreme Court ruled that states could not restrict a prisoner's right to file a writ of *habeas corpus*, asserting the right of a person in custody to appear in court so that a judge can determine whether he is being legally detained. As late as 1956, however, a federal court ruled: "Courts are without power to supervise prison administration or interfere with the ordinary prison rules and regulations," and added in another case eight years later that "supervision of inmates . . . rests with the proper administrative authorities and . . . courts have no power to supervise the management of disciplinary rules of such institutions." In other words, the court denied prisoners the rights that non-prisoners were guaranteed by the Constitution.

The door swung open wide at last in 1966 when the U.S. Court of Appeals ruled against the use of "strip cells," isolation cells without furniture, toilet facilities, or running water where prisoners were confined completely naked. The court declared that

> civilized standards of humane decency simply do not permit a man for a substantial period of time to be denuded and exposed to the bitter cold of winter in northern New York State and to be deprived of the basic elements of hygiene such as soap and toilet paper. [Such] subhuman conditions . . . could only serve to destroy completely the spirit and undermine the sanity of the prisoner. The Eighth Amendment forbids treatment so foul, so inhuman and so violative of basic concepts of decency.

About the same time the courts began paying more attention to prisoners, a perfect storm of upheavals in American society sparked a historic increase in the prison population. One was the emergence of illegal drugs as a cultural force. Though these drugs had been available for many years, the 1960s marked the first time that popular music, movies, and even professors at respected colleges, glorified drug use and encouraged the population to break the law and indulge themselves.

Another dramatic change was the wholesale rejection of God in the public square. Beginning with the Supreme Court ban on school prayer in 1962, a series of rulings removed Christmas displays, religious symbols, and even the Ten Commandments from places where they had been for generations. This trend went against a tradition dating back to the Mayflower Compact of 1620, which the Pilgrim settlers signed aboard the Mayflower before they set foot on American soil, stating that one of their chief objectives in coming to the New World was the "advancement of the Christian Faith."

As late as 1938 the U.S. Supreme Court affirmed that the United States was "a Christian nation," though as such it welcomed citizens of all faiths and of no faith at all. In 1956 Congress officially designated "In God We Trust" as the national motto. Whereas government had resolutely supported religion up to the 1960s, government by the 1980s was ridding itself of every meaningful vestige of religious expression.

Without what William Bennett later called the "moral compass" of shared absolutes, public moral standards dissolved into a confusion of relativism: "If it feels good, do it." As long as Americans had recognized general overarching assumptions about right and wrong, a public standard of behavior could make them think twice about violating them. In marginalizing moral judgments, public institutions removed a powerful deterrent to bad behavior.

Another issue of the times was the change in perceptions about the causes of criminal behavior. President Lyndon Johnson introduced his Great Society welfare programs in the 1960s in response to the thinking that members of the social underclass were "victims of society." These people broke the law and lived in poverty, Johnson declared, not because of their personal decisions, attitudes, and actions, but because of an uncaring system that denied them what they needed to succeed. If they were criminals, it wasn't their fault.

In response, state and federal governments instituted a massive welfare system to give this constituency housing, education, medical care, child support, and other benefits. Ultimately the U.S. government would spend three trillion dollars on antipoverty programs over forty years only to see the crime rate skyrocket.

Frustrated with the prison system's failure to rehabilitate inmates, state governments in recent years instituted mandatory sentencing and "three-strikes-you're-out" laws to keep repeat offenders behind bars longer. With prisons already dangerously overcrowded, these laws pushed the prison population to critical levels and spurred an unprecedented round of inmate lawsuits and new prison construction.

By the time Chuck Colson started thinking about prison reform based on Christian principles, the penal system he confronted was the product of nearly two hundred years of flawed policies and trillions of misspent dollars. His only resources in the face of this daunting challenge were unflinching resolve, a small circle of dedicated friends, a few political contacts in high places, and the faith that God was guiding him.

Between their first Washington Discipleship Seminar in November 1975 and the incorporation of Prison Fellowship nine months later, Chuck and his circle of advisors worked their way through painful mistakes, refined their curriculum, celebrated the joys of men and women finding new lives in Jesus Christ, and prayed fervently that God would guide them and the inmates they hoped to reach. Washington seminars were the backbone of Prison Fellowship in its early years, and in time led to new and even more effective tools for the future.

[CHAPTER 5]
D.C. Disciples

When Colson first contacted Dick Summer, the chief of federal chaplains, about releasing prisoners to come to Washington for Bible seminars, Summer insisted that his chaplains should pick prisoners to be furloughed. Chuck disagreed, fearful that this would discourage inmates from wanting to come. Chuck didn't oppose furloughs, he opposed letting chaplains, as members of "the system," choose prisoners to be furloughed. He knew from his own time behind bars that prisoners were always suspicious of anything promoted by "the system," and wanted members of Fellowship House, along with respected, successful Christian businessmen who lived in cities closest to the prisons and supported their reform, to select the participants.

When Summer dug in his heels, Colson argued even more strongly. Colson's ace in the hole was that he knew Norman Carlson, who as director of prisons was Summer's boss, was willing to let Chuck make the final selections. Eventually Summer agreed to allow volunteers from Fellowship House to choose from a list of prisoners recommended by their chaplains, with Fred Rhodes and Chuck making the final cut.

The first group numbered twelve prisoners in all, six black and six white, two of them women.

Chuck spent part of the morning of their arrival on November 2, 1975, walking alone along the Potomac, praying that everything would go well. There would be no cells, no guards, nothing to keep these prisoners from giving in to the temptation to escape. Summer had given him his emergency phone number, saying, "Call us, not the police, when—I mean if—there's trouble." By 7:45 p.m. that night all twelve inmates were safe at their quarters at Good News Ministries, but if any one of them disappeared over the next two weeks, Chuck knew the whole program might collapse.

Chuck opened the seminar with a prayer, then explained to the men and women exactly what they'd be doing. They were being equipped to go back to their prisons and lead their fellow inmates to God behind bars. God could not only make their incarceration bearable, He could redeem those lost years. He could forgive them no matter what they'd done, as long as they believed in Him and truly repented. He could free them from drugs and any other addictions. He could comfort their families and help heal the wounds of separation. He could prepare them for success on the outside, rather than drifting back to the habits that landed them in prison in the first place. Most important of all, He could offer them eternal life in heaven.

Harold Hughes spoke next. He reminded his audience—still looking a little shell-shocked by their temporary freedom—that they weren't there to play and have a good time. "You are here to learn what it means to be disciples who deny everything else in the world for the sake of Jesus Christ. If you have any other thoughts in your mind, get rid of them." He also made the point that he had been jailed in six states for drunkenness. He and Chuck weren't better than any of them, he said, but they could teach from a point of experience.

Chuck added some thoughts to close out the evening. He reminded the twelve inmates that they represented the whole American prison population. If this experiment worked, it would eventually improve the lives of all prisoners; if they failed this prison constituency, Chuck warned, their hopelessness would continue.

The next morning Fred Rhodes drove the inmates in a van to Fellowship House for their first Bible study. Chuck began with the question of what "fellowship" actually was. For people who had spent years in prison, it was an alien concept. The unwritten code of conduct in prison was that everybody kept to himself: don't make other people's problems your problems, don't fight anybody else's battles, and don't try to be somebody's buddy. Though most of these prisoners were already Christians, it would be a big step to go from believing in Christ to sharing that belief. Doing so broke two of the unwritten rules: don't appear weak, and don't butt in.

Doug Coe then spoke on "Who is Jesus?" Again the basics were familiar, but Doug drew from his own experience and involvement with the Young Life ministry to help the inmates see Christ as a person-Redeemer, a true Father. Since so many prisoners come from homes where the father is absent, the meaning of God as Father is hard at first to absorb.

Another speaker that first day was John Staggers, a black ministry leader who was already taking Christian outreach into the prison in nearby Lorton, Virginia, for the Fellowship Foundation. Staggers had shared his doubts with Chuck that prisoners would go for a program developed by a big shot like him. When Chuck reminded John he was a big shot who had also gone to prison, that had calmed his fears.

Though some of their study skills were rusty at first, the student inmates eagerly absorbed the lessons, studying Scripture, exploring their own Christian experiences, and learning how to share their faith in the closed world of prison without offending others or causing trouble. The students even asked to give up their free time after the first week's classes to witness in the nearby Arlington County Jail. One big, beefy seminar student named Soul led two convicts to Christ that afternoon in the maximum security unit. Before it was even finished, the seminar was already yielding fruit.

During the second week Chuck arranged for the inmates to visit Senator Lawton Chiles of Florida, noting, "I am sure it was the first time that twelve convicts ever gathered in the office of a U.S. senator." Another senator strolled in during the prisoners' visit. Startled to hear that these clean-cut guests in street clothes were inmates, he was deeply moved by their stories of faith. That night the visiting senator and his wife prayed that Jesus Christ would come into their lives as He had come into the prisoners'. Reflecting on that story Chuck exclaimed, "How often God chooses the powerless to touch the mighty!"

The final meeting of the first Washington seminar, on November 15, was a combination awards ceremony and communion service. For some of these prisoners, it was the first time they had ever earned an award for anything. They treasured the simple certificates Chuck handed them as signs of a great personal victory. The sense of celebration was contagious among the circle of people who knew about the seminar and its goals. Fellowship House had squeezed 125 chairs into a room that could comfortably hold 100, yet more than 200 guests came to watch the festivities, spilling out into adjacent rooms and onto the floor.

One prisoner summed up the general feeling when he said, "I've learned a lot these two weeks about prayer, fellowship, and what a disciple of Jesus is supposed to be. I feel clean inside, as though a lot of dirt has been drained out of my system. For the first time in years I believe I can give love to others and receive it." As they returned to their prisons the next morning, another inmate added, "I do not go back as a prisoner but as a disciple on a commission for Jesus Christ."

Between his speaking engagements and preparations for the publication of *Born Again*, Chuck eagerly planned another Washington seminar. Norm Carlson had actually agreed only to a pilot program, but Chuck forged ahead as if it were an open-ended opportunity and no one made any move to stop him.

Chuck naturally supposed things would be even smoother the second time around. On top of the fact that they now had some experience, he and his team also had a new pair of willing hands. Paul Kramer had been one of Chuck's closest friends when they were prisoners together. The Bible studies and prayer sessions they organized at Maxwell were in fact the models for the training Chuck was doing at Fellowship House. He had seen how Christianity changed the lives of men around him and knew what an encouragement they had been to him—an island of light and hope in the sea of hopelessness that was prison life. Chuck had worked months to help Paul get out on parole, and finally the parole board agreed to release him to the Good News Mission for the last three months of his sentence.

But not everyone was convinced that the training seminars had long-term potential. Paul, for one, wondered about Chuck's commitment to the future. When the second group of discipleship inmates arrived, Chuck asked Paul to take charge of them for the two weeks.

"And then what?" Paul asked. It was a fair question. At that point Chuck didn't know himself what God had in store for him in the long run.

John Staggers was even less enthusiastic about a second seminar class. He felt like an outsider, he said, taking orders rather than having a fair say in planning the ministry activities. He had been ministering in the Lorton prison for two years on behalf of Fellowship House and was apprehensive that his work there would be overshadowed by Colson's take-charge manner and national profile. Colson and Staggers met one day at Fellowship House with Harold Hughes, Doug Coe, and Fred Rhodes to talk it out.

"The one group was okay," Staggers said. "But, man, I don't think this is going to work if you want to keep doing it month after month."

"This isn't my program, John," Chuck answered, "it's for the Fellowship. I'm willing for you to take it over."

After some more discussion, the group saw that they had to be of one mind about their ministry, working together in the name of Christ, before they could move forward. They decided to continue with a second class as planned, but not schedule any others until the five of them agreed on what to do and how.

The second discipleship class began on February 15, 1976. It did not go well. The tone was set the first night that the fourteen participants met at the Good News Mission. One of the two women in the group, a gorgeous young former fashion model convicted on drug charges, showed up wearing a see-through blouse and no bra. Harold Hughes ordered one of the women volunteers to take her out before the night was over and get her something more modest. Later in the week, another inmate admitted he was using drugs; his frequent absences and dilated eyes had given him away. Unlike the first class there were numerous minor rule violations. The study sessions were slow and tedious compared with the animated give-and-take of the first group.

One of the few bright spots in the class was the other woman, a soft-spoken former bank officer named Jackie Butner. Convinced that her male colleagues earned more than she did for the same work, she resorted to what she admitted was "creative accounting" to make up the difference. Jackie's faith deepened noticeably during her two weeks in Washington. She also helped make sure her sexy classmate wore decent clothes every day. When several of the students spoke at the graduation ceremony it was her "eloquent statement of faith," Chuck said, "that touched hearts most deeply."

In evaluating the results of the second class, Chuck saw that when he was making the final selection of prisoners, he had been too distracted by other events, including the run-up to the release of *Born Again* (on February 18, three days after the seminar started). He and the others also decided they needed an outside teacher, someone not part of the Fellowship House group, who could focus more fully on preparing the lessons. And from here on out, there would be no mixed groups; the classes would be all men or all women. Most significant of their problems, Chuck believed, "was the dampening of the Holy Spirit through our disunity."

In the months that followed, Chuck continued to struggle with whether or not to enter Christian service full time. *Born Again* was hugely successful, bringing him a new round of notoriety and shining a very public spotlight on the prison problem in America. But while he was drawn to the needs of prisoners, he was simultaneously repulsed by the memories they stirred of his own miserable prison experience.

Yet when planning for the third seminar began, the process went more smoothly than ever. John Staggers declined Chuck's offer to give up the ministry, and decided to leave the seminars in order to spend all his time ministering at Lorton. Paul Kramer took charge of getting furloughs for the participants. In a welcome change from the second class, when prison authorities had challenged every prisoner the fellowship selected, the next class breezed through the approval process.

George Soltau, a third-generation Reformed Presbyterian minister from Dallas, volunteered to teach. In addition to his solid evangelical credentials, he also had years of experience in prison ministry. He knew how to deal with the low self-image and hopelessness so many prisoners experienced that made it hard for them to open their hearts to Christ.

The third class, conducted in May, was the best yet in terms of dedication and leadership potential. The following month Chuck left for his extended book promotion tour overseas. His experiences on that trip— seeing the surge of popular interest in Christian ideas and prison policy his book produced—helped guide him to the decision he made later that summer on the Oregon coast to incorporate Prison Fellowship.

His high public profile made it natural to think Chuck's operation would be called Charles Colson Ministries. Advisers insisted that putting his name up front would help with publicity and fund-raising. But Chuck insisted his work would not be celebrity driven. He wanted "a movement of God's people in fellowship." The focus was on prisons and on fellowship, both among prisoners and among Christians. Prison Fellowship it was.

By the time the fourth Washington Discipleship Seminar started in August, the ministry had refined and clarified its goal "to take Christian leaders out of prison to receive intensive discipleship training so that, upon their return to prison, they could disciple and impact the lives of other Christian inmates to build the church of Jesus Christ on the inside." Paul Kramer added that they worked toward that goal by forming "small cell groups of prisoners nurturing one another."

Chuck pledged his royalties from *Born Again* to help get the ministry up and running. The first Washington seminar had been funded courtesy of Fred Rhodes's credit cards. All the members of that class were from prisons near Washington because there was no money for airfares. Now the ministry could set up a modest office and operating budget independent of Fellowship House.

Though Colson was the public face of Prison Fellowship, he had neither title, position, nor pay in the beginning. Fred Rhodes was the ministry's first president. Before heading the Postal Rate Commission, he had been deputy director of the Veterans Administration. In 1974, the year Chuck was tried and imprisoned, Fred took early retirement and wrote to Chuck that he would help with the Lord's work wherever he was needed.

The nucleus of PF's leadership team continued to strengthen. Another key figure was Gordon Loux, formerly public relations director for Moody Bible Institute, whom Colson had met at a book convention during the rollout of *Born Again*. Loux impressed Colson with his grasp of the evangelical publishing business. The two wrote back and forth for about a year. Despite their shared interest in prison ministry, Gordon and his family were comfortably settled in Wheaton, Illinois, and he and Chuck both wondered whether a new and untried ministry such as PF could offer him a career.

Within a month of Prison Fellowship's founding, Loux felt the Lord leading him to service in Washington. Along with his wife, Beth, and their three sons, he pulled up stakes and moved east. Providentially, Colson's great friend and Christian brother Harold Hughes was moving to a farm in Maryland and selling his house in Virginia for just what the Loux family could pay. In less than a year, Loux was elected senior vice president of the ministry.

Jackie Butner, the convicted embezzler who had so impressed Chuck and the other leaders as the standout student of the second seminar class, became the ministry's first full-time secretary and accountant. When somebody wondered if the job might be too much of a temptation for her in light of past offenses, Chuck responded, "Possibly so, but the whole ministry [is] based on trust." With Chuck and Paul Kramer, that made three ex-offenders in the group. Paul was happy to move into a permanent office in Arlington, modest though it was. Until then he had worked out of his bedroom at Fellowship House, bounding down two flights of stairs every time he had to take a phone call.

Along with Fred Rhodes, Chuck welcomed a few other trusted Christian friends into the leadership circle. Graham Purcell, a faithful prayer partner during Watergate's darkest days, joined the board of directors, as did Neal Jones, Chuck's pastor and friend who had re-baptized him after his release from prison. Among the other members was Myron Mintz, a confidant and former law partner who had managed the Colson family finances while Chuck was in prison.

Other men and women literally showed up on the doorstep offering to work only for expenses or to volunteer their time. One was Mike Cromartie, a recent college graduate willing to work as a researcher for expenses only. His full beard made him a suspicious character in Colson's eyes, as he recalled in *Life Sentence:* "There was a time when I associated young, bearded men with antiwar pot-smoking hippies, but Mike turned out to be an answer to prayer. Bright, studious, and energetic, he began to organize a library, prepare research and speech materials." Later Mike became Chuck's frequent travel companion and stayed with the ministry through its early years.

Lisa Whitney was another dedicated volunteer who came early and faithfully stayed on. She was teaching school in Milwaukee when she read *Born Again*, and she wrote to Chuck volunteering her time during summer vacation in exchange for a place to live. For her first two weeks in Arlington she didn't have an office, but she stayed on until she had to return to the classroom that fall. The next summer she volunteered again, and the third year she left her teaching job to work full-time for PF.

The office was crowded but, in Lisa's view, the close quarters added to the excitement. "We had Bible studies sitting on the floor," she later recalled. "And everybody wore a lot of hats. There was so much to do— so much opportunity—and so few of us to do it that we all pitched in wherever we were needed." Jackie Butner, in addition to her office duties, became an effective PF spokeswoman to ladies' organizations. "There was a sense of involvement and connection in those years that was so exciting," Lisa added. "We all could feel the pulse of the ministry because we were all so close to it." (Thirty years after her first volunteer summer, Lisa is still with Prison Fellowship as field director for Wisconsin, the ministry's longest serving employee.)

From the earliest days, Prison Fellowship focused on encouraging local church members and pastors to volunteer their time to teach and counsel prisoners, then supplying those volunteers with the training and materials they needed. Compared to other organizations of similar size and scope, PF remains a lean organization with relatively few paid staff (about four hundred in 2006). The ministry never raised up rank upon rank of Prison Fellowship employees to carry out missionary work in the field. It equipped church volunteers for most jobs, both to keep costs down and to avoid competing with the churches for manpower and financial support. Coming alongside congregations in this way placed both the church and the ministry in their biblically mandated roles: the church bringing God's teaching to His people and Prison Fellowship assisting the church.

Churches were enthusiastic and dedicated colaborers with PF from the first. The District of Columbia Baptist Convention helped sponsor the three Washington seminars held before Prison Fellowship was officially founded, and it supported others to follow. Beginning with the eighth seminar group, area Presbyterian churches added their shoulders to the wheel, supplying meals, meeting space, and other assistance. In the first year, Prison Fellowship and church volunteers trained seventy inmates in Washington and sent them back to start Bible study and prayer groups in their prisons.

Visits from government officials in Washington became a high point of the seminars. Participants called on Christian members of Congress to share their testimonies. These meetings gave prisoners a forum to discuss their struggles as Christian inmates and gave lawmakers what was often their first up-close look at incarcerated men and women. In the eyes of these Washington heavyweights, inmates were transformed from faceless statistics into real human beings.

Director of Prisons Norman Carlson commissioned a study to see what difference the seminars made. Dr. Daniel Peterson led a team of psychologists that interviewed prison chaplains and seminar participants in seven prisons. They reported,

> Every chaplain we have talked with is totally sold on the Fellowship House program. Inmates who have participated in the experience have almost universally been instrumental in turning the institutions' religious programs around or revitalizing existing programs. This appears to be a valuable and dynamic ministry.

This encouraging report made it all the more surprising when, in the spring of 1977, Prison Fellowship faced a crisis that threatened to bring the whole ministry to a screeching halt. George Ralston, warden of the federal penitentiary in Oxford, Wisconsin, had refused to grant a furlough to any of the inmates PF wanted for their next seminar class. Statistics indicated that the longer a prisoner had left to serve, the more likely he was to try to escape. Warden Ralston thought all his chosen inmates had too much time remaining.

Paul Kramer took the call from Ralston, and then shared the news with Colson. Chuck didn't seem worried at first and suggested they simply replace the Oxford prisoners with men from another facility. But Paul thought otherwise. Ralston, he observed, was a leader among federal wardens. If he refused to let his prisoners come to Washington, others would follow suit.

"Imagine," Paul continued, still fuming, "telling us we should move into his prison." Taken by surprise, Colson asked if the warden was really serious. "Of course not," Paul shot back. "It was a clever ploy to get me off his back."

In a meeting later that day, Fred Rhodes boldly suggested they call Ralston's bluff and agree to teach a seminar inside the prison. Paul dialed the warden and made the offer, then returned minutes later with shocking news: "Ralston called *our* bluff. We're to go to Oxford in three weeks."

That day marked a historic fork in the road for Prison Fellowship. One path, as we shall see, led to in-prison seminars, which over time became the ministry's principal outreach, while the other path continued along with the Washington Discipleship Seminars.

Impressive though Dr. Peterson's report on the results of the Washington seminars was, Chuck, Paul, and the others kept looking for ways to make them even better. One variation was the Wilderness Seminar, a pilot program developed in 1978 by PF vice president Ralph Veerman. Inmates spent the first week camping in the Wisconsin wilderness, testing their faith, building their confidence, and learning to trust each other. The second week combined Bible study and leadership training with mentoring inner-city youth. In theory, the program combined a series of appealing activities under one umbrella; in practice, the inmates returned to their prisons exhausted and sore. After long discussions and heartfelt prayer, Chuck decided to end the Wilderness Seminars.

Another variation was spending week one in Washington and week two at Ligonier Ministries, R. C. Sproul's ministry headquarters in Pennsylvania. Sproul was an important theological mentor to Colson during the early years of Prison Fellowship, and Chuck wanted to share his rich and valuable teaching with the inmates.

In the fall of 1978, Paul Kramer handed over management of the Washington seminars to Lisa Whitney, who was then heading the in-prison programs. By 1985, when Lisa moved to another position in the ministry, more than five hundred prisoners had graduated from the Washington classes.

As in-prison ministry and a host of other programs flourished, PF considered from time to time whether the original Washington seminars were still a productive use of time and resources. A 1982 pilot study showed that prisoners who took the Washington training tended to have lower rates of re-incarceration than a control group without it, but the study recommended a more detailed research project.

As taking seminars into the prisons gained momentum, Washington seminars became a smaller part of the overall Prison Fellowship picture. The ministry could stage any number of in-prison seminars simultaneously almost anywhere, anytime, as long as there were enough volunteers to teach them. It was far easier to get those volunteers into prison than it was to get the prisoners out. And it was far more cost-effective to hold classes in prison chapels or dayrooms than it was to fly a dozen inmates to Washington and cover their room and board for two weeks.

Over time there was a gradual shift in emphasis in the Washington seminars away from training Christian leaders to teach Bible studies in prison and toward raising the churches' awareness of prisoners' spiritual needs. The modified seminars had inmates spending time with volunteer families and sharing their testimonies with school groups. While the community emphasis had its benefits, some PF leaders believed, as Paul Kramer said, that the heightened awareness "was accomplished at the inmates' expense," since they received less nurturing and attention than before.

In 1990 the Institute for Religious Research reported that graduates of the Washington seminars between 1976 and 1979 were substantially more successful in later years, with lower recidivism, a longer crime-free period following release, and a decrease in crime severity. More detailed findings revealed that the success rate varied with demographics. The best results were in low-risk prisoners and women; seminars had little impact on black males. The study concluded overall that PF was meeting its objectives "by helping a significant number of prisoners become productive members of society."

But by the time the Institute made its report, the classic Washington seminars had been remade in a different form, serving a different purpose. Concerned with security even though no prisoner had ever tried to escape, the Federal Bureau of Prisons mandated that only inmates with less than a year remaining on their sentences were eligible for the seminars. That meant graduates would have but a few months at the most to make an impact on their prison communities.

In 1988 there was only one Washington Discipleship Seminar, coordinated with the National Prayer Breakfast and the subsequent Prison Fellowship donor retreat for key supporters of the ministry. The focus there was more on public relations than on inmate leadership training. As a later internal analysis observed, "In essence, the true purpose of the program became diluted." A similar seminar in 1990 was the last of the line.

A 1991 postmortem reported that the Washington Discipleship Seminar program "was ended because of the high cost to operate it and the apparent lack of enthusiasm of PF national office staff." Despite this harsh self-assessment, a task force that met in the fall of 1987 pre-served the essence of the Washington seminars for a while longer as a state-level ministry. The revised program was christened as IMPACT and was launched in Oklahoma and Delaware a year later. The new program was a one-week intensive leadership curriculum including a one-day public service project and a dedication and graduation service.

As a much smaller cog in a vastly larger ministry, IMPACT never achieved the notoriety of its Washington predecessor. But the Washington program catapulted Prison Fellowship from a vision in Chuck Colson's shaving mirror to a living, breathing ministry that set the stage for all that followed.

[CHAPTER 6]

Challenges Met

In transforming from an ad hoc prison outreach under the Fellowship Foundation umbrella to an established nonprofit corporation with its own offices, donors, and objectives, Prison Fellowship survived some serious strategic blunders. The ministry aimed to cover new ground in prison reform, but much of that ground was jealously protected by entrenched bureaucracies. In this alien environment, even Chuck Colson's keen sense of perception and highly developed political skills couldn't keep his new organization from embarrassing setbacks.

In a 1996 interview celebrating Prison Fellowship's twentieth anniversary, Chuck thought back over the challenges of those early years and decided, "Probably the biggest bonehead move I made was trying to put PF chaplains in all of the prisons. . . . We thought we could do the job better than anyone else. . . . That was a major miscue." It's true that the ministry ran into a hornet's nest of opposition at the time, but the lessons learned paid important dividends in the long run.

Encouraged by the success of the PF Washington Seminars, director of prisons Norm Carlson made a proposal in January 1977 to mesh Prison Fellowship even more directly with the federal system. The prison chief offered to let Prison Fellowship put its own chaplains in a new federal penitentiary opening soon in Memphis. "There just aren't enough funds for all the programs we need there," Carlson explained. "The chapel program is going to be hurting, and so I was thinking maybe you could find the support to hire the chaplains and put them in, for a while anyway, until we get more money."

Chuck shared his response to the offer in *Life Sentence*. He instantly imagined that a PF chaplain on the inside "could turn a prison into a spiritual retreat center." Colson quickly said yes, though he had no men in mind to fill the positions and no way to pay them. Two days after his meeting with Carlson, speaking at the National Prayer Breakfast in Washington, Colson explained the new opportunity in Memphis and said he believed the man for the job was in the room at that moment. After the breakfast a man passed him a card: "Bill Beshears, Minister of Education, First Baptist Church, Warner Robbins, Georgia." On the back were the words, "I may be the man." And he was—ordained, experienced in prison ministry, energetic, masculine, and an ex-con who had been sentenced to probation for forgery in twelve states.

Because of the large black population in Memphis, and the emphasis inmates place on their racial identity in prison, Chuck and others at PF prayed for a black chaplain to assist Beshears. Soon afterward they hired Jesse Ellis, a young, enthusiastic African-American who was an adjutant of the Church of God in Christ.

When Bill Beshears began his ministry in Memphis on March 15, Prison Fellowship still had no permanent source of funds for his salary. Chuck's book royalties and the donations that were beginning to come in barely supported the Washington seminars and the modest ministry headquarters in the Arlington basement. To get financial commitments for the Memphis ministry, Chuck and Fred Rhodes spoke before a civic group luncheon in Memphis on April 29 that drew an audience of twelve hundred. Their response was an exhilarating confirmation of the Fellowship vision: the room pledged two-thirds of the annual budget on the spot and two hundred people volunteered to mentor prisoners with counseling and Bible study. Adrian Rogers, pastor of Bellevue Baptist Church, the city's largest, accepted the post as honorary chairman.

But turf wars and political minefields lurked just over the horizon. Prison Fellowship had already alienated some chaplains by insisting that PF select the Washington seminar classes. In his excitement to explain to his Memphis audience what a breakthrough it was having a PF-supplied chaplain in prison, Chuck thoughtlessly criticized and generalized about prison chaplains, reliving his own prison experience as he spoke:

> I know what it can mean to those men inside to have someone they can trust. In the prison I was in, the visiting chaplain was a military officer stationed at the air force base. He was a fine decent man, but a friend of the warden and no inmate would confide in him. Government-paid chaplains are part of the system and the system is the "enemy" to most inmates.

He then repeated a story he'd heard about a prisoner who went to confession and admitted his role in a murder. The priest turned him in, and the inmate was eventually executed.

The story was more fiction than fact, but by the time Chuck knew the truth he was caught up in a storm of protest from chaplains and a flood of complaints, real and imagined, from inmates. Newspapers picked up the story. The Catholic archdiocese threatened to withhold the sacraments in the prison unless a government-paid chaplain came in. Protestant organizations took offense as well, with one church official reminding Colson, "We've got a lot of jobs at stake, you know."

Chuck's sincere and profuse public apologies helped save the Memphis program. A rousing speech by Harold Hughes to a conference of federal wardens in Fort Worth on the power of Christian brotherhood also made giant strides in repairing the political damage. But what really kept Memphis going were results. A third of the prison population there signed up for Bible study or fellowship meetings. Chapel services were packed, and more outside volunteers signed up to help than Chaplain Beshears could get permission to bring inside.

One of the most compelling testimonies in Memphis came from a prisoner Chuck visited in solitary confinement (invariably called "the hole" in the prison world). The inmate encouraged Chuck to stick with his chaplains through the controversy. Chuck asked him why.

"Thirty-two years I've been in prison," he answered. "I've been beaten, tossed in the hole over and over, better off if I had been dead. Jesse and Bill are the first people in thirty-two years who cared for me. I'd give my life for those two." He paused. "Mr. Colson, I've come to believe in your Jesus through them."

By the time Chaplain Beshears started his new job, Prison Fellowship was hard at work on another opportunity that could dramatically demonstrate the power of Christian discipleship behind bars to an audience of millions. The publicity and royalty income from *Born Again* had been a lifeline for the young ministry. To leverage that essential financial and public relations tool even further, Chuck and the rest of the leadership team investigated the prospect of adapting the story to film. The big question was whether to make it as a "Christian" film or try for a general audience in partnership with a Hollywood studio.

"Billy Graham wanted to do it," Chuck recalled, "but he couldn't make a decision about what he wanted to spend." A feature film produced to Hollywood standards would require a huge investment: stewardship was a big consideration for both organizations. The two men had long talks about how they might collaborate on the project. The Billy Graham Evangelistic Association had a film production and distribution arm, World Wide Pictures, up and running with a history of successes reaching Christian audiences and a sizable catalogue of releases. "We knelt and prayed together on the floor of a Memphis hotel room," Colson continued. His reliance on prayer at that juncture was consistent with every step he had taken since the ministry began. If God wasn't in it, Chuck wanted no part of it. In the end, the Billy Graham organization and Prison Fellowship decided not to move forward together.

After further discussion and prayer, Colson, Fred Rhodes, and Hollywood producer Robert Munger agreed to make an independent picture for release and distribution through a Hollywood studio. It was truly an act of faith: no major Hollywood company had ever distributed an overtly Christian film, and no one at PF knew how God would provide the three million dollars they needed. The ministry's entire budget for the coming year was less than half a million dollars.

Washington businessman Paul Temple began assembling a syndicate to fund the project. For a while it seemed like the financial goal was too ambitious. At a point when the fund-raising appeared hopelessly plateaued, Chuck shared his concerns with a young driver who was taking him from an airport to a speaking engagement in North Carolina.

"How much do you need from each person?" the driver asked.

"A hundred and fifty," Chuck answered.

"I'll take one."

Chuck smiled. "I mean 150 thousand."

"I know. I'll take one."

Three more investors bought shares that same weekend, then one underwriter pledged the remaining shortfall. By God's providence, the deal was done and production could begin. *Born Again* as a movie would, in Chuck's words, enable Prison Fellowship "to strengthen our work significantly as we reach out to thousands hungering for the Good News." By the summer of 1977 the production company had signed an agreement with Avco-Embassy, one of the biggest motion picture distributors in America, to release the movie nationwide.

Though outwardly optimistic and upbeat throughout two years of discussion, scriptwriting, and production, in private Chuck was appalled by the process of turning his book into a film. "I had certain control, but not complete control" over the movie, Chuck said. Screenwriter Walter Bloch submitted a script that seemed to Colson predictable and overwritten.

The situation deteriorated even further when principal photography began in Washington shortly before Christmas 1977. Colson could scarcely bear to see his story so convoluted. It wasn't pridefulness that made him insist on changes, but concern that the project might ultimately do the ministry more harm than good. "There were times when I said, 'If you can't fix this I'm going to break up the film.' And I would finally get my way. It was an agonizing process." The atmosphere during the shoot disappointed Chuck as well. "There was a great deal of immorality on the set," he said.

Of the finished product Chuck admitted, "It was a big disappointment." Yet even as a so-so Hollywood effort, the movie *Born Again* introduced the story of Prison Fellowship to many thousands of people who would never have heard it otherwise. It gave churches a rallying point to help raise up volunteers for PF programs and increased the general awareness of PF. This publicity produced a surge of new volunteers across the country.

The film blazed a trail as the first-ever Christian Hollywood feature, and for all its artistic shortcomings earned an 84 percent "very good" or "excellent" rating from preview audiences. Eighty members of Congress attended the gala premiere at the Kennedy Center in Washington on September 24, 1978, along with thirty members of the diplomatic corps and thirteen inmates who had just completed the fourteenth PF Washington seminar.

Though ticket sales proved disappointing, stories from behind the scenes showed God at work in unexpected ways. Film and Broadway star Dean Jones, who played Colson, had been through a conversion experience of his own. Rich and successful after a string of lead roles in Walt Disney movies and the musical comedy hit *Company*, he had tried to fill the emptiness in his life with parties, drinking, and driving race cars. Finally, he found peace and fulfillment in Christ. At a press conference, Jones said his own journey made it possible for him to portray the "spiritual reality" of Chuck's story, adding, "If my experience will provide a background for the Holy Spirit doing something worthwhile or showing something in depth of what has happened to change Chuck's life, then I'll feel that I've performed my function properly in the picture."

There was real-life drama too in the story of actor Jay Robinson, who played Colson's law partner, David Shapiro. His portrayal of Emperor Caligula in *The Robe* had earned him a spot on *New York Times* critic Bosley Crowther's list of ten best movie performances of all time. Then Robinson turned to drugs, spent fourteen months in jail, and saw his career grind to a halt. To support his family he took a job as a fry cook. When *Born Again* was casting, he tried out for a small part, but ended up with second lead. Before the production was over, his heart was pierced by Colson's personal saga, and he knelt in Bob Munger's office asking the Lord to take over his life.

In addition to its general release, Prison Fellowship used the *Born Again* film as a teaching tool in prisons, helping audiences of offenders understand who Chuck Colson was and why he had dedicated his life to prison ministry.

As the history of Prison Fellowship (or at least a version of it) was being chronicled by a Hollywood film crew, the future of the ministry was being cast by Warden George Ralston in Oxford, Wisconsin. What seemed at first a serious blow to Prison Fellowship in the spring of 1977 actually led to a whole new level of ministry, reaching far more inmates with the gospel of Christ than the Washington seminars could ever have done.

Ralston had vetoed seminar furloughs for every inmate that Prison Fellowship picked to attend the next Washington class, and he suggested instead that they come to his prison and teach the seminar there. The next day Paul Kramer traveled two hours by car from the nearest commercial airport to Oxford, where five hundred men lived "as cut off from the world as a leper colony," in Chuck's words.

They had three weeks to pull all the pieces into place, most importantly a body of volunteers who would continue the Bible studies and counseling after the seminar sessions were over. Paul identified people in the sparsely populated region who would step up to the task: a young couple who had already visited the prison as volunteers, a Christian bookstore owner, a farmer and a small-town pastor who shared a burden for prison work, plus a few women from a Bible study group. Four Christian businessmen from Minneapolis flew in to help as well.

Reverend George Soltau of Dallas, who taught the Washington Seminars, spoke the first three days, followed by John Jolliffe, a consulting prison psychologist in California. Colson closed the seminar on Friday, reaching the team's headquarters in a truck stop motel the night before, after a long week of speaking engagements.

Despite the preconception among prisoners that Christianity was "sissy" and a refuge for weaklings, ninety-four inmates signed up for the Oxford seminar and eighty completed the full week, including ten Black Muslims, one of whom made a profession of faith. A Muslim stood up after Chuck's remarks and said, "All my life I've been looking for something. Well, I never thought I'd find it in prison, but this week I have. It is love. It is the love of Jesus Christ right here."

Staff members from other prisons came to observe the program, including some who strongly opposed Prison Fellowship encroaching on their territory and implying government-paid chaplains couldn't do their jobs. A failure at Oxford would resonate throughout the prison system; at worst it could imperil the whole ministry. But as PF enthusiastically reported, God did a great work that week in Wisconsin. Warden Ralston's succinct appraisal was typically straightforward: "This has been a tremendous week. You should do this in every prison.

I'll recommend it if you want." That April week in 1977 established the prototype for what became the core ministry of Prison Fellowship: teaching about Christ behind prison walls with the help of local volunteers, local support, and local follow-up.

Also that week, the story of Prison Fellowship first intersected with the life of a man whose journey is a bittersweet reminder that prison ministry is a difficult and sometimes heartbreaking calling, and that things happen in the world that are beyond man's power to understand.

Herman Heade holds a historic place in the story of Prison Fellowship. He was a prisoner in Oxford, Wisconsin, whom Warden George Ralston refused to release for the Washington seminar.

Even though he came from a broken family in the Black Bottom ghetto of Detroit, Herman Heade had big plans for the future. As a boy, he dreamed of playing major league baseball with the Detroit Tigers. His dad imagined him winning an appointment to West Point. All those optimistic visions faded when Herman fathered a child at seventeen. To escape his father's disapproval and make a fresh start, Herman enlisted in the army the next year and shipped out for Vietnam. He came home with two medals, but underneath that decorated uniform was a wayward and unsettled heart.

Herman landed a unique opportunity back in civilian life: he became the first black draftsman ever hired by North American Rockwell, a giant defense and aerospace company. But he fell short of his potential, drinking and carousing after hours and ultimately leaving his family to move in with a girlfriend. When he realized his lifestyle took more money than his paycheck could ever provide, he robbed a store. The take was less than one hundred dollars.

Emboldened by drinking he tried again, holding up a bank with a toy pistol and walking out with twelve hundred dollars. Quickly arrested, he was convicted and sent to the state prison in Jackson, Michigan, where some of the five thousand inmates taught Heade plenty he didn't know about criminal life.

Out on parole, Herman landed a job as a correctional officer at a school for juveniles. "They thought I was reformed," Herman explained, "but I jumped right back into living the old way again, and [still] couldn't support my lifestyle on my paycheck."

Less than two years after his release, Herman walked into a bank with a fake bomb. The tellers cleared the lobby, stuffed six thousand dollars into an attaché case, and handed it over. Herman headed straight for the airport and took a flight to San Francisco.

Three months later, broke and lonely, he came back home only to have his estranged wife send him packing. He bought a .32 automatic and checked into a hotel. Sitting on the bed, alone, afraid, and desperate, he thought he heard a voice say, "Pull the trigger. God will forgive you."

Instead of obeying the voice, Herman called his father. Together they called the parole officer and within hours Herman was back in prison with a charge of extortion added to his rap sheet. He spent ten months in solitary confinement, alone in a cell twenty-three hours a day. Released back into the general prison population, he was sitting on a bench talking with some other inmates when the prison librarian dumped a bunch of books out of a bag. Herman continued the story:

Digging through them I found one called *Peace with God* by Billy Graham and tossed it on the floor. Another prisoner picked it up and said, "Herman, you ought to read this one." I tossed it away again. Later back in my cell, there was that same book on the floor. I'd tossed it over my shoulder into my own cell.

This time he started reading it, and after a while he was "bawling uncontrollably." Remembering the moment, he said, "I was supremely happy inside because I'd been born again. It was like chains had come off my mind. I sat there saying 'Praise God' again and again, thanking Him for finding me, for giving me peace. It was incredible."

He tried to explain what had happened, but none of the other inmates could understand. Neither could his dad. Only his mother seemed to have a feel for his spiritual transformation. At the trial for his third robbery, he also told the judge about his newfound faith. Though the judge seemed impressed, he still sentenced Herman Heade to ten years in Oxford.

That was where he first heard about Prison Fellowship. He joined a weekly Bible study and was chosen to go to Washington for a discipleship seminar. Because he had so much time remaining on his sentence, Warden Ralston denied his furlough. But what seemed like a deep disappointment became the catalyst for historic change when Prison Fellowship came to Oxford in April 1977.

Herman made a strong impression on Chuck Colson during the in-prison sessions. Colson recognized his sincere faith, leadership ability, and clear potential, and personally invited him to come to Washington after his release. Eighteen months later he was on the Prison Fellowship staff. By then he had finished a correspondence Bible school curriculum and had been ordained.

Early in 1980 Herman headed back to Oxford, this time as an in-prison instructor. Nearly eighty inmates signed up for the course, many of them attending out of curiosity to see if the Herman Heade they knew as a prisoner was really now teaching the Bible. When the seminar was over, they knew more fully what had transformed Herman's life—and what could transform their own. "It was a high point of my spiritual experience," Herman said in an interview. "They knew my experience with Christ was real. They had seen me carrying a Bible as an inmate. Now two years later I was still carrying one. They knew God's work in my life was valid."

Herman also returned to Jackson and Milan, the two other prisons where he had served time. There again he had the joy of sharing Christ with men who were where he once was, encouraging them by example and proclaiming the love of Jesus.

But in a tragic turn, Herman later slipped back into the severe depression that had brought him to the brink of self-destruction years before in a Detroit motel room. This man who on the outside had progressed so far from his criminal past could not finally escape the deeply rooted hopelessness within. In 1991 he ended his own life. It was a reminder that God's plans are not our own, and that His ways are not always clear. Herman's many friends could only thank God for his life and work, and have faith that what they saw as sadness and evil, God could use for good.

But in that hope-filled spring of 1977, there was no hint of the sadness to come. The Oxford seminar was an unqualified triumph. Before Colson and his associates left town, they had already begun planning a seminar at Sandstone Federal Prison in Minnesota. That session began on June 19, with enthusiastic support from Warden Max Mustain and thirty community volunteers in and around Minneapolis. Opening the seminar, Chuck received a standing ovation from inmates and the families of prison staff members who attended. More than one hundred inmates, nearly a quarter of the prison population, took part.

Miles Lord, a federal judge who heard Colson speak at a prayer breakfast earlier in the morning, went to the prison that afternoon to see for himself how Colson's ideas translated into actions. Addressing a jam-packed chapel audience, Judge Lord told them, "I could issue an order cutting all of you loose tonight"—here he was interrupted by loud applause and cheers—"but it's more important for you to be right here. All I can do is save your butts. God can save your souls. I've been around prisoners a long time, and I've tried out a lot of programs to help these men. Let me tell you my conclusion: Only God can change a man, and that's the message of this evening."

At the end of the week, one prisoner summed up the transformation in his perspective: "You think we are in prison? We aren't; we're in Utopia." An assistant warden observed, "I have worked in the system for eighteen years, and I have never seen anything like what happened here this week."

CHAPTER 7

God Behind Bars

Oxford and Sandstone were prototypes for the ministry that would in time carry Prison Fellowship and the love of Christ through the doors of virtually every prison in the United States. Under the chaplains' oversight and with the wardens' cooperation, PF leaders presented a week of Bible studies and activities designed to encourage imprisoned Christians and reach out to non-Christians. Local volunteers led study groups, helped with logistics, followed up with participants once the seminar was over; and donated money to fund the program.

If Oxford and Sandstone set the template for in-prison ministry, Chuck Colson's riveting words to a tense and threatening prison crowd later that year solidified the ministry's message. Atlanta was in the grip of a withering heat wave when Chuck accepted an invitation from newly appointed warden, Jack Hanberry, to hold a seminar at the federal penitentiary there. The Atlanta prison had a violent history of organized crime activity on the inside: ten men murdered in sixteen months, including one burned to death in his sleep. Two thousand convicts festered in a hundred-year-old fortress built for twelve hundred men, without air conditioning, and in some places, without fans. The inmate power structure was testing Warden Hanberry. His first two months on the job he saw two murders and twenty-four fires. As a former prison chaplain, Hanberry believed a PF seminar was his best chance to keep the inmate population under control.

There were only eight professing Christians in the whole place. Nevertheless the prison chaplain, Charlie Riggs, managed to recruit 150 inmates for the seminar. In a surprise move, Warden Hanberry decided to open Colson's speech on the last day to the whole prison. For a maximum security facility like Atlanta, any sort of large assembly was rare because of the riot risk. It had been years since the entire population had been allowed to congregate in one place.

By the time Colson walked from the entrance gate to the chaplain's office to pray with the tiny core of Christians before his speech, sweat was running down his face. Cal, the unofficial leader of the Christian group, warned Chuck not to preach or talk about Jesus. The men wouldn't stand for it. No religion. Somebody in the circle suggested talking about prison reform. Chaplain Riggs agreed and had it announced that reform would be Colson's topic.

The heat and the tension were almost unbearable as Chuck sat waiting for his turn to speak. The eight hundred or so inmates in the auditorium were restless and inattentive. The tension was almost unbearable. Chuck jotted down some quick notes on prison reform, but as he listened to a prayer from a priest named Tim Ondahl, he had a flash of inspiration. "We thank you, Father, for the fine people here this evening to share with us," Father Tim was saying. "They bring dimensions to us that we never dreamed possible. They don't even expect a payback. And, for us that is unreal; or maybe, we should say simply Christian."

Chuck described what happened next. "Down in the front row was one of the toughest inmates in the prison. 'Joe the Butcher,' they called him. He sat there scowling, his arms crossed in front of his chest. As I looked out at that rough crowd, I realized that these guys did not need to hear about criminal justice reform. They needed to hear about Jesus."

Standing to speak, the room buzzing with chatter and his clothes soaked with sweat, Chuck tossed his notes on prison reform aside, took off his coat, dropped it to the floor, and spoke from the heart words he was sure came straight from the Holy Spirit: "I know what you guys are thinking. What is Chuck Colson doing here? What is his game? Is he here to make money? There's got to be an angle, right?" Heads nodded all around as the men grumbled their agreement.

Chuck traced the history of his vision to bring men out of prison, how God had miraculously opened the doors to changing not only the system, but the prisoners' lives as well. The room grew quiet as Chuck continued softly, his voice breaking with emotion, perspiration dripping from his face.

"A lot of you think of Christianity as those nice, white, middle-class, good people in the good part of town who never get into trouble and go to church on Sunday. . . . You say they don't know what it is to be in prison. And you're right. Most of them don't."

Chuck went on to tell them about a man who was a prisoner just like they were. "Jesus Christ is the prophet of the loser. I am a loser just like every one of you here in this room. We're all losers.

"Jesus rode into Jerusalem on a donkey. He did this so that people would know that He came from the dirt and the mud, that He has been with weak and ordinary people and those who hurt and suffered. The message of Jesus Christ is for the imprisoned—for your families, some of them who aren't making it on welfare on the outside. Christ reached out for you who are in prison because He came to take those chains off, to take you out of bondage. He can make you the freest person in the entire world, right here in this lousy place.

"Jesus had been a prisoner," he said, "He'd had His friends rat on Him, spent time in solitary, was stripped, told to cop a plea, had gone to death row." These were experiences inmates could relate to. Heeding the Holy Spirit's prompting, Chuck shared fervently that Jesus had suffered for them because He loved them.

His voice gradually grew louder. He became emphatic, almost shouting, his arms waving, his hands chopping the air.

"Jesus, the Savior, the Messiah, the Jesus Christ I follow is the One who comes to help the downtrodden and the oppressed and to release them and set them free. This is the Jesus Christ to whom I have committed my life. This is the Jesus Christ to whom I have offered up my dream and said, 'Lord, I want to help these men because I have lived among them. I came to know them; I love them. There is injustice in our society, but we can change it. Yes, God, we can change it. I give my life to it.'"

For an instant there was absolute silence. Then a roar filled the stifling room as inmates yelled, clapped, shouted with joy, and stood on their chairs—many with tears rolling down their faces.

"I can't tell you how incredible it was," Colson said. "I felt the Holy Spirit come on that place. People were galvanized. When it was over, they started coming down front. . . . Joe the Butcher came forward and repented of his sin and gave his life to Christ. Later that night I went to a Motel 6 with our staff. I sat up most of the night praying and rejoicing. The prison ministry had been going for a year, but perhaps that was when it was really born."

It was, Colson said later, "the first time I really preached the gospel in prison." Sixty-five inmates participated in the seminar; many more signed up, but there wasn't room for them. With minor tweaks and changes, it was the message he delivered in prison for decades to come. In his book *Life Sentence*, he added, "Prisons do not reform individuals; people rot and decay inside. . . . Change and reform begin with changed hearts." Everyone in the Atlanta Penitentiary that night learned the truth of those words. In the middle of a tumbledown prison, where murders were commonplace and hope a distant dream, the message of God's love and forgiveness brought tears of joy to scarred and sweat-stained faces that had not felt them in many years.

In his speeches and writings, Chuck consistently pointed out that Prison Fellowship depended on Christian volunteers to take the lead in conducting in-prison seminars, to keep programs going once the seminar week was over, and to follow up with prisoners after their release. As Colson explained, "Our dream is to enable outside-the-wall Christians to join hands with imprisoned Christians and thereby shine the light of the gospel into every dark corner of every institution." PF could never field a paid staff big enough to make a dent in prison ministry on a wide scale; whatever happened would come by God's grace through His people in the church.

Small and lean though it was, by the end of 1978 Prison Fellowship was a million-dollar operation, including $600,000 in donations and a $214,000 net gain from premieres of *Born Again*. That year Colson and the board of directors restructured Prison Fellowship. As the balance shifted from Washington-based programs to programs in the field, the ministry needed a staff presence on the ground in the communities they served. With revenue growing and the future bright, Prison Fellowship hired seven regional directors to administer the work so they could coordinate directly with criminal justice officials, local churches, inmates, and volunteers the programs brought together. These seven covered Prison Fellowship activities in 130 cities. Chuck's ultimate goal was to reach all 600 communities in the country where there were prisons. The Washington staff enthusiastically supported this organizational change, though they felt somewhat disconnected at first when regional directors took the reins of local ministry and outreach.

Also in 1978, Fred Rhodes resigned his position as the first president of Prison Fellowship, and the board of directors elected Chuck Colson to replace him concurrent with his role as chairman. Now Colson would lead day-to-day operations as well as long-term strategic development, while also continuing his role as the public face and voice of Prison Fellowship.

A story prepared for *Jubilee*, the Prison Fellowship newsletter, is an accurate snapshot of his message during those years. He insisted that most prisoners were "incarcerated on the misguided assumption that the prison experience will rehabilitate them, deter others, and do things that society expects its justice system to do. Experience proves that this assumption is simply wrong." The high repeat offender rate demonstrated that prisons didn't rehabilitate. Punishment, he noted, was theologically sound, but "it backfires on society when offenders are degraded, sexually perverted, morally twisted, depersonalized, and have their families and futures shredded into a midden of rancid memories." It was not the type or the brutality of punishment that deterred crime, he said, but the certainty of punishment.

To many people a prison sentence meant justice was served, Chuck continued, but as taxpayers, "crime victims spend tens of thousands of dollars a year to keep robbers in prison. They're robbed twice." And prisons provided "only temporary safety for society." Most prisoners upon their release "tragically become more of a threat than before." The result: a net loss in safety.

As the ministry gained momentum, it became more aware of the importance of its organizational image. For the first few years of its history, along with no permanent home and not enough furniture, Prison Fellowship had no corporate symbol or logo. There's no evidence that the ministry leadership thought much about it early on, but a heartfelt statement by a PF board member set the wheels turning that eventually produced a design identifying Prison Fellowship around the world.

Ligonier Ministries founder R. C. Sproul served for a time on the Prison Fellowship board. Chuck credited Sproul with "jump-starting" his knowledge of Scripture, saying, "No one has discipled me more." He admired R. C.'s evangelical Christian theology and worldview, and the two had spent time together at Sproul's study center in the Ligonier Valley of Pennsylvania, an experience Colson later called one of the most profound of his Christian life, praising Sproul's "exceptional learning, brilliant mind, and inimitable personality."

In 1979 Sproul accompanied Colson on a visit to Stillwater Prison in Minnesota. It was his first time inside any prison, and it made a lasting impact. At a dinner for Prison Fellowship supporters that night, R. C. told the audience,

> What I saw today will remain with me all my life. Those men inside were hurting, suffering; there was agony in their faces. And yet hope came to them, even to them who are the 'bruised reeds' of whom Isaiah spoke. Even these [prisoners], marred as they are by a lifetime of sin and hurt, even these He will not break. In His gentleness and compassion, the Jesus Christ of whom Isaiah prophesied comes especially for the very sinful, the very hurt, and the bruised of this world.

Sproul referred to the promise of God in Isaiah 42: "I will put my Spirit on him and he will bring justice to the nations. A bruised reed he will not break, and a smoldering wick he will not snuff out. In faithfulness he will bring forth justice; he will not be falter or be discouraged till he establishes justice on earth." (Isa. 42:1b, 3–4)

Prison Fellowship ministered to the "bruised reeds" in prison; the bruised reed in Isaiah captured the ministry's mission. A new logo depicting this imagery first appeared on the 1979 annual report; soon letterhead, business cards, and signs sprouted it as well. Though modified slightly over the years, it has remained the symbol of the ministry and a constant reminder of the people it serves.

Even for prisons as deadly and hostile as the Atlanta Penitentiary in 1977, crises behind bars seldom drew national headlines. But at about the time Prison Fellowship adapted as its symbol the bruised reed God would safeguard, a horrific tragedy reminded the world of how desperate, sinister, and violent prison life could be. Before dawn on February 2, 1980, a mob of inmates took over the security control center at the

New Mexico Penitentiary in Santa Fe. Badly overcrowded and frustrated by a prison culture that promoted "snitching"—the hated practice of informing on a fellow prisoner—the attackers wanted revenge.

With too many prisoners and too few staff as a result of state budget cuts, the prison had abolished the inmate council and other lines of communication between offenders and corrections officials. This deprived inmates of an essential safety valve for expressing their views. It also cut off an important tool officials had used to gauge the mood of the prisoners, check out rumors, and generally keep their finger on the pulse of the inmate population. A later investigation revealed the administration had become so dependent on snitches that a chaplain reportedly told an inmate, "My son, God wants you to be a snitch."

The inmates at Santa Fe had no specific grievances or even any leaders directing their actions. As *Corrections Magazine* reported in its follow-up investigation, "The inmates, leaderless and uncontrolled, went berserk." No hostages were killed, and the prison was retaken without firing a shot, giving New Mexico officials an evident victory in the standoff.

The horror came when authorities entered the prison thirty-six hours after the uprising began and found scenes that according to one report, "rivaled some of the sights encountered by Allied troops who had liberated Nazi concentration camps at the end of World War II." Thirty-three prisoners had been horribly mutilated and murdered by their fellow inmates. Alleged informers were "burned to death with blowtorches, castrated, hacked apart, and decapitated." Hundreds more were raped and tortured.

Though Prison Fellowship had no program in place at Santa Fe, it was a nightmare scenario for the ministry. Just as PF was gaining firm traction and national recognition, a sudden tragedy so brutal could swamp its message, invalidating its claim that tighter control was not the solution, that the answer was spiritual renewal from the inside.

People looking for God behind bars, even in such a tragic moment, saw Him in the Christian prisoners who carried wounded inmates outside to safety at the height of the violence. These prisoners faithfully went back into the carnage for more injured men instead of escaping during the confusion. Local Prison Fellowship volunteers brought food and blankets to friends and family members as they kept vigil outside, with prisoners' families and staff families waiting and hoping together. After order was restored, PF volunteers interviewed every inmate inside and contacted each man's family.

Writing in *Jubilee*, Chuck voiced his concern that this terrible event would cause a public backlash against prison reform and reinforce the lock-'em-up strategy he himself had once so confidently endorsed. He exhorted the public to take two lessons from the Santa Fe riots. First, that prisons are dangerous places—all the more reason not to lock up nonviolent offenders (typically about 70 percent of a prison population) in a cellblock with rapists and murderers. "Many of the men killed there did not deserve to be in prison," he wrote, "or they at least deserved as much protection from dangerous criminals inside prison as society demands on the outside. To sentence them to the same compound with dangerous criminals is, in my judgment, a brutal form of cruel and unusual punishment. Almighty God holds us accountable for it."

The second lesson he underscored was that prisons make prisoners worse, not better. "Prisons are just producing tougher criminals who earn a veritable PhD in crime while behind bars. Every statistic about crime proves that." Americans, he insisted, had to get rid of their "frontier vigilante attitude about crime and punishment."

A Justice Department study in the wake of the tragedy reported that the Santa Fe prison was "one of the harshest, most punitive prison environments in the nation." Summarizing the results in *With Liberty for Some*, author Scott Christianson concluded,

Officials now acknowledged that the place had long been notorious for its nepotism, totally untrained personnel, corruption, filth, unsanitary and uncomfortable living conditions, fire hazards, sexual abuse, escapes, and violence; a place where mentally disturbed inmates were kept in plaster body casts with holes to allow them to defecate and urinate.

If there was no serious public backlash in the aftermath of the Santa Fe riot, neither was there any groundswell of support for new ideas, especially from the politicians. Speaking to the New Mexico state legislature soon afterward, Colson made an impassioned case for prison reform. The lawmakers couldn't deny the facts, but one of them replied afterward with unusual candor, "Thank you for coming, but to be perfectly honest, you're the kind of person we try to avoid. This is not a very good issue politically."

The national scope of the Santa Fe crisis gave Prison Fellowship a high-profile platform to present its position on prison reform, adding a new sense of urgency to the message. Chuck redoubled his admonition to Christians to get involved as prison volunteers, write their elected officials in support of prison reform, and most of all steer civic leaders toward restitution, halfway houses, community service, and other alternatives to prison sentences for nonviolent offenders.

Later that year, on November 6, 1980, Colson took his message of freedom in Christ to the largest prison in America. Angola Prison, built on the site of an old Louisiana plantation, was not only the biggest, but also had one of the longest average sentences in the country. Colson had quite a warm-up act that day—country music legend Johnny Cash. Two thousand men sang along with Cash as he delivered a string of his classic hits. Also in the audience was Governor David Treen, visiting the prison for the first time ever.

When his turn came, Chuck surprised his listeners by asserting that Christ endured a situation a lot like their own, expanding on the theme he had first sounded in Atlanta:

Jesus Christ experienced everything ever experienced by any prisoner, anywhere. He was betrayed to evil men by an informant—a snitch—

from His closest circle of friends. He was put through the mockery of a fixed trial and given the most unjust sentence ever handed down by a court. He was strip-searched by His guards, mocked by them, and spat on by them. His friends and family fled.

Beaten and abused, He was forced to carry on His own back the instrument of His execution—a rough wooden cross. He was tortured, and then put to death in one of the most painful ways imaginable. On either side of Him were thieves. One of them even mocked Him.

In offering up the sacrifice of a perfect life, Jesus made our human nature whole and well, conquered our human sin and guilt, and earned for us all the everlasting mercies of Almighty God.

Looking out at a sea of desperate faces forgetting their desperation for the moment, Chuck saw many tears as the men roared their appreciation for so hopeful a message in so hopeless a place. "Imagine that!" they seemed to answer. "Jesus was a prisoner too!"

CHAPTER 8

Molding the Message

Describing the growth strategy for Prison Fellowship, Chuck Colson observed, "Practically nothing we started was planned." That was surely the case for the in-prison seminars. Chuck and a few others had three weeks to slap together a curriculum for them. But perhaps, when combined with the unwavering faith that they were following God's calling, the spontaneity helped them win supporters. PF didn't have time to worry about failure or to consider a range of options. They just had to get on with it.

Nevertheless, promoting prison ministry remained a challenge. Even after the positive publicity following Santa Fe and Angola, Prison Fellowship still encountered resistance from corrections officials who looked at outside visitors as an unnecessary security risk as well as an inconvenience. Building bridges to prison staff, particularly in light of Chuck's unintentional but costly dust-up with the chaplain corps, was crucial for gaining access. Though he didn't flaunt it, Colson's friendship with the top man in the federal system served him well in getting into places for the first time. Ralph Veerman, vice president for ministry services, summed up the local wardens' position: "Even though they were fairly hostile to Colson as an ex-con-outsider-Christian 'born againer,' prison officials didn't want to mess with Chuck because he was close to Norm Carlson."

For all the impact in-prison seminars have had over the years, their content is simple and straightforward. There's no great secret revealed, no great theological knot untied, no psychology of the criminal mind analyzed and dissected. The lessons focus on fundamental needs and the challenges inmates face both in prison and when they get out. They present an alternative to the ingrained habits that lead most ex-cons back to crime and back to prison. And they specifically address the most basic needs of men and women behind bars: how to survive in prison; how to hold on to their faith and share it with others; how to stay out of prison in the future; how to make an honest living; how to manage conflict; how to be accepted and loved by their family and friends; and how to be forgiven. Prison Fellowship's objective is to point them toward Jesus Christ as the only source of answers and the strength to hold on to them.

Prison Fellowship seminar materials are simply written. More than half of adult prisoners in America are functionally illiterate; they can't fill out a job application or balance a checkbook. The rest of the incarcerated population read at a seventh-grade level on the average. The Bible teaches that the lessons of Christ are so simple even little children can understand them. Therefore telling God's truth in the simplest form takes away nothing from its power and impact.

Most important of all, Prison Fellowship seminar lessons are lessons of the heart and spirit. Rather than hammering away at the idea that people shouldn't take drugs and shouldn't steal, which every prisoner already knows, PF cuts through the actions to the motivations behind them. People won't take drugs if they believe it's wrong to take them. In PF's teaching, wisdom and change come not from scolding or threats, but from knowing and following the example of Jesus.

Prison Fellowship seminars are both realistic and hopeful. They don't pull any punches when it comes to the consequences of individual responsibility. But at the same time, the tone is supportive and encouraging. Prisoners are wary of authority and tend to resist being told to believe or act a certain way. PF presents the gospel and invites participants to consider it on their own schedule, in their own way.

A typical seminar is completed in five two-hour sessions over a weekend, led by trained volunteer leaders with permission from the prison chaplain and warden. There's plenty of leeway in the format to account for local chapel services, meal schedules, and times during the day when prisoners have to return to their cells and be counted. The average class size is about fifty inmates, broken down into discussion groups of six or eight.

The seminars cover presentation of the gospel, learning to live in a prison environment, discipleship training, building family relationships, and preparing for release. The leader's guide for volunteers describes teaching the class as

a creative presentation of the Gospel and Christian principles. . . . A seminar is not a preaching service and is not like teaching a Sunday school class. You will want to use a variety of creative teaching methods such as small group interaction, individual participation, object lessons, and music. You'll need to be alert, cautious, and dependent on prayer and God's power.

The most basic of all the seminars, and one of the most popular, is called "Surviving and Thriving." It teaches newly incarcerated prisoners how to adjust to prison life, explaining the stages they're likely to go through and comparing their situation with the life of Joseph in the Bible.

New inmates, particularly first-timers, are almost universally resentful, lonesome, and afraid. For them success in life was probably measured in possessions, money, and their social position in the neighborhood or gang. Suddenly, all that has disappeared. They have no status, no identity. Nothing is familiar. In its first session, "Surviving and Thriving" explains that in Christ they can have an abundant and joyful life even in prison. God is everywhere, all-forgiving, and ready to make the toughest struggle bearable.

Inmates learn the story of Joseph in Genesis. His brothers were jealous of him because their father favored him, and so they kidnapped him and sold him as a slave. His new owners took him to a strange land. Through all this, Joseph felt God's presence. Because of his favorable attitude and also because he could interpret dreams, Joseph was purchased by the Egyptian pharaoh. Eventually Joseph earned the pharaoh's respect to the point that he was put in charge of the entire royal household. So here he was, freed from his unfair imprisonment because of his attitude and faithfulness.

But then he was falsely accused by the pharaoh's wife and thrown into prison again. Again, he faithfully kept his hopeful attitude and waited on the Lord. When the pharaoh recognized Joseph's ability interpreting dreams, he placed him second in command of the whole kingdom. During a famine, Joseph's father sent Joseph's brothers to Egypt to buy grain, not realizing Joseph, whom they all thought was dead, had earned a powerful and responsible position. The brothers bowed down to Joseph, once enslaved, now the master of everyone except the pharaoh himself. Rather than being vengeful, Joseph was gracious and generous. He was there to save his family from starvation. What man intended for harm, God intended for good (Gen. 50:20).

"Joseph demonstrated how our response to what happens in our lives is a choice," the lesson explains. "He could have been angry with his brothers. But instead, through God's power, he showed them love." Inmates write down what about their own situation reminds them of Joseph's.

"Surviving and Thriving" examines five stages prisoners usually go through during their first weeks in prison. The relief fairly glows on their faces as the lesson unfolds—somebody knows how they feel! The prisoners realize that they aren't weak or crazy; they're normal. And they learn that through faith in Christ they can know peace and contentment, even in such an inhospitable place as prison.

Stage 1: The person realizes change is coming. He may be awaiting sentencing or waiting for the prison term to start. Life seems the same as before, the environment familiar. He's sure of his reputation, responsibilities, friends, and enemies.

Stage 2: The shift to prison is imminent. Conviction and sentencing take away the prisoner's status and position and attracts attention, small talk, and gossip. His responsibilities fade away, and he begins to separate himself from friends and family. He may become withdrawn and emotional.

Stage 3: The inmate enters prison. How he deals with his feelings during this transitional time sets the stage for how prison will affect him from now on. He has no status or identity either in or out of prison. Responsibilities and relationships on the inside are unclear. He's cut off from people on the outside, but he hasn't had time to build relationships on the inside. He feels like a number. He may be fearful, apprehensive, angry, lonely.

Stage 4: Prison is the new reality. The inmate learns the routines of prison life. He looks for a group to be part of, establishes his identity with prisoners, prison staff, and others. He is often touchy, fearful, and easily offended.

Stage 5: The prisoner is settled in the new environment with new friends, new expectations, and a new identity.

The smooth way through these stages, the seminar explains, is the way of Christ. The Lord can use any circumstance, even being in prison, to make us more like Christ. A relationship with Christ makes us approach the transition to prison a different way. Our status, relationship, and peace in Him are the same whatever the environment: "Regardless of our changing status in other areas of our life, once we have repented and received Jesus Christ as our Savior, our status in Christ remains constant. Our position in God's kingdom is assured. We belong to Christ." God delivers us from anger, fear, and bitterness; Jesus Christ is the rock.

The lessons also encourage new inmates to resist the temptation to give in to a life dominated by fear. They should submit to legal authority as Jesus did, knowing they are under His watchcare. But they will have to decide whether to cave in to inmate strongmen and follow their lead, or to stand fast for what is right in God's eyes. The choice is theirs to make: live for Christ or live for themselves. As the seminar booklet explains, "You can either hold on to anger, fear, discouragement, and unwillingness to submit, or depend on the Holy Spirit" who gives you power to walk with Christ. Not only can offenders survive in prison, they can thrive there.

Another popular seminar, "Christian Basics I," clarifies Christian fundamentals for believers. This session encourages people who've temporarily abandoned their Christian walk, and encourages non-Christians to make a first-time commitment by exploring:

- **What salvation is and how to know it is theirs.** As 2
  Corinthians 5:17 joyously explains, "Therefore, if anyone is in
  Christ, he is a new creation; the old has gone, the new has come!"
  Anyone can be new in Christ no matter what he has done.
- **Why and how to read the Bible.** The Bible is God's roadmap
  to and through the Christian way of life, true for all time and
  all people who want to know and obey God. Study it regularly,
  carefully, and humbly with an open mind.
- **What prayer is, how to pray, and why it's important.**
  Prayer is one-on-one discussion with the Creator. It isn't
  demanding favors from God, or something to do only in a crisis,
  but it is humble, bold, faithful, and honest. God hears every
  prayer, but He doesn't always give us the answers we want.

- **How to share the Christian faith with others.** Share personal experience while pointing not to the person, but to Christ. As ambassadors for Christ, Christians should pray, plant the seeds (by their own actions, casual conversation, etc.), present the gospel honestly and naturally, and listen carefully.
- **How to grow as a Christian.** Christ calls us to be part of a fellowship of believers. There are no "Lone Ranger" Christians. Encourage other prisoners who want to live as Christians by helping them apply seminar lessons, keeping them accountable, and praying for them.

In January 1992, Prison Fellowship volunteers at Mississippi State Penitentiary conducted the five-thousandth in-prison seminar. What had seemed a crushing disappointment in 1977—Warden Ralston's refusal to send an inmate to Washington was now bearing rich fruit. After inmates responded enthusiastically to a seminar at Southern Michigan Prison, officials there asked Prison Fellowship to stay on-site permanently. It was the first time a prison had invited PF to operate, not just during seminars, but to supervise and coordinate continuing ministries full time.

As one flint-faced Michigan inmate explained,

> I always thought that I would keep on hating people until I just burst with pure hate. My first day at the seminar my heart was as cold as ice and mean as a mad animal. [When I found out] there are a few people who care about a person like me, then I knew it was time to change my ways. There's no life more complete than to have someone care for you, and then to have God care.

Another seminar graduate wrote, "For twenty-six years I have lived a life of pure anguish. But today as I sit in my cell, I have such a feeling of peace and love. Thank you for helping me find my way home.

Your seminar started a spark in many of our lives, and this flame will never die."

To attend Prison Fellowship seminars, inmates usually sign up through the chaplain's office. But some members of the prison community don't qualify to attend: those offenders in the infirmary, in the hole (isolation), or on death row. Since early in his ministry, Chuck Colson has always asked to talk with the men in these places when he visits a prison. In the hole or on death row, inmates communicate through ventilation grates or pass-through slots in their doors. A visitor may have to sit on the floor to have a conversation. Part of these inmates' special punishment is that they are never allowed to mix with the others or to attend special programs including Bible studies or chapel services.

Prison Fellowship has seen how these men—usually abandoned by their families, outcasts among outcasts in prison, often with absolutely nothing to pass off the hours—needed the comfort and assurance of Christ. Men on death row are some of the neediest: sentenced to die, facing the end of life and whatever lies beyond it alone.

Prison Fellowship wanted to bring Christ's message to death row. But their path was littered with hurdles. Since the inmates there were already sentenced to die, there was no way prison staff could threaten them to keep them in line, no privileges they could withdraw for breaking rules. Mixing condemned men with outsiders was extremely risky.

And yet, on the strength of PF's track record and Colson's skill in persuading the authorities, the impossible happened. The weekend of September 18, 1981, the first ever death row seminar took place at the Holman Correctional Institution near Atmore, Alabama. It was the first time in the history of the prison that the whole death row population was allowed to assemble in one room. The fifteen men there, plus Prison Fellowship leader (and ex-con) Herman Heade, the prison chaplain, and the chaplain's assistant were locked in a room together for five hours at a time.

Convicted murderers, these men were desperate to know someone remembered and cared about them. They drank in the message of Christ like travelers in the desert. It absorbed their pent-up hatred at the world and the system, easing their attitude and in some cases dramatically improving their behavior. At the end of the seminar the inmates and instructors shared communion together. Seeing the difference the experience made to the men, the chaplain at Holman made Bible study available on death row from then on.

Hundreds of thousands of American prisoners speak only Spanish, but for years Prison Fellowship had no formal programs for them. Not only do Hispanics struggle with all the difficulties any prisoner has, they face language barriers and an alien culture. Many have no family at all in the U.S. And the rate of illiteracy for Spanish speakers is even higher than for the general prison population.

A historic crisis prompted Prison Fellowship to broaden its outreach to Hispanics. In 1981, Fidel Castro released thousands of inmates from Cuban prisons and asylums and sent them sailing toward the United States in what became known as the Mariel boat lift. American authorities rounded up sixteen hundred of the most dangerous criminals among the refugees and locked them up together in an Atlanta prison.

Prison Fellowship responded with its first ever Hispanic seminar the weekend of October 19–22, translating study materials into Spanish and enlisting Hispanic volunteers to present the Christian message. Though virtually all of the Cubans were nominal Catholics, many of them combined their worship with elements of Caribbean folk traditions or voodoo. The PF seminar marked the first time most had ever heard the unaltered biblical version of Christianity.

Though the program and the audience were different from anything else Prison Fellowship had done, the result was familiar. Many prisoners who were angry, frightened, separated from their families, prone to violence, and thrown into a foreign culture (which their totalitarian leader had taught them to hate for a generation), were transformed.

Certainly there were lawbreakers and dangerous men among them, but because of what they learned through PF their outlook changed, and their behavior as a group became calmer and safer. Mirroring the aftermath of the death row seminar, PF's success led to regular weekly Spanish Bible studies with volunteers in the Atlanta prison. To the Scripture study, they added English lessons and culture and life skills training.

Where chaplains or wardens were not inclined to approve in-prison seminars, a good alternative was a Bible study. Since they didn't take any special scheduling or resources, PF Bible studies were easier for skeptical prison authorities to accept. It was also a familiar concept in most cases. Local volunteer laymen and ministers had led studies in prisons long before Prison Fellowship was active, though according to Ralph Veerman, "many of them had a lot of problems with access."

Largely on account of Colson's Washington connections and personal experience, PF worked at first with federal prisons, which hold only about 10 percent of the country's prison population. As the ministry expanded, PF volunteers went more into state prisons as well. If there were already church groups holding Bible studies inside, PF supported them to whatever degree they wanted. Often those volunteers joined the expanding force of men and women who used PF training and materials in their classes. As PF attracted more volunteers, the ministry fielded a national team of staff supervisors to train and assist them, and the studies expanded in some cases into more formal mini-seminars.

In order to keep refining and improving its programs, Prison Fellowship regularly assessed its materials and methods and interviewed prisoners, corrections officers, volunteers, and others to track results. In the late 1980s a ministry task force concluded that prisoners needed more support in making the transition to freedom. In-prison seminars and Bible studies dealt only with the spiritual dimension of life. Prisoners needed help applying their spiritual lessons to everyday life—finding a job, setting a budget, identifying goals.

Al Quie, one of Colson's original Watergate prayer group members, founding PF board member, and former governor of Minnesota, proposed the idea of matching individual prisoners nearing their release dates with volunteer mentors who would help them through their last few months in prison and their first few months in the free world. Quie, elected president of Prison Fellowship in 1988, helped lead development of a new program called Life Plan Seminars.

These sessions encourage inmates to take responsibility for past choices and set goals for the future. The mentor's role is critical in the transition process; he meets with the inmate monthly for six months before release and weekly for six months after. Part of the mentor's goal is to set up a resource network with members of his church who can help the ex-prisoner find a place to live, a job, transportation, Christian friends, and other resources.

Mentors and other volunteers remain the backbone of Prison Fellowship. Today volunteers all undergo twelve hours of formal training in order to uphold the ministry's standards and maintain good relations with prison officials. Another part of the process is to show volunteers how to make their prison seminars fun as well as meaningful, using everything from zany rap videos to skits, puzzles, and games. The training proved so successful that some state officials requested that all volunteers from religious organizations should take PF training.

Volunteers who represent Prison Fellowship must also reflect eight core values of the ministry:

- Centered in Jesus Christ—in our obedience to the Risen Lord
- Grounded in the Bible—in our life and ministry
- Dependent on prayer—as the foundation for ministry
- Partnered with the church—as the biblical means for ministry
- Committed to unity—with all believers in Jesus Christ as our Lord Jesus commands

- Compelled to evangelize and disciple—to bring Jesus Christ to the lost and to help people to grow in Him
- Loving others—by treating all people with grace, trust, and respect
- Seeking excellence—by demonstrating integrity and wise stewardship

Volunteering for prison ministry can be an exhilarating experience for the volunteer as well as the prisoner. Bert Owen knew all about that feeling. When the doors of Limestone Correctional Center in Limestone County, Alabama, opened in 1982, Bert was one of the first volunteers through the gate, excited at the prospect of sharing his faith with men who needed it. Many of his neighbors had opposed construction of the new prison and fought to have the project cancelled. But Owen, a retired engineer, circled the site on his Schwinn ten-speed, praying for a Christian warden to run the place.

During his first visit to the compound, he approached a circle of black prisoners and started a conversation. "We prayed and sang and had a beautiful time with the Lord," he said. But his second visit to start a Bible study was not so easy. He asked the assembled group of twenty, half black and half white, to join hands in prayer. The blacks and whites refused to touch each other. When Owen explained, "To start a church here, you've got to start loving each other," ten men walked away. Next week the same group met again, and Bert made the same request. This time the circle joined hands. Bert believed God had shown him a miracle.

When Bert heard that PF was coming to conduct an in-prison seminar at Limestone, he and his wife, Elsie, signed up to volunteer. One of his students was Big Ed; at three hundred pounds he lived up to his name. He told Bert he was hostile at first to the whole idea of Christianity and Christians: "I hated your guts the first time I saw you. I just wanted to slap you and the other goody-goodies carrying around Bibles." But to the Owens' delight Big Ed came to Christ through their teaching. "And if I ever get out," Big Ed said later, "I'm still gonna be serving Jesus. Thank God for Bill and Elsie. They're the only two people in the world who didn't give up on me."

From its earliest issues, *Jubilee* shined a spotlight on volunteers. The 1990 PF National Volunteer of the Year, Dick Mitchell, started out as a very unlikely prospect for the honor. Dick was a small business owner and taxpayer, who was appalled to learn in 1985 that the average cost of housing an inmate at the prison, a mile from his shop, was almost thirteen thousand dollars a year. He had two suggestions for the authorities: hand out guns and knives to all the prisoners and let them solve the overcrowding problem, or have two prisoners share a single bed, with one working while the other slept.

A local meeting of prospective Prison Fellowship volunteers changed his mind. Impressed by the invitation of area director Myles Fish to extend the hand of compassion to prisoners, ex-prisoners, and their families, Dick volunteered to lead Bible studies, discussion groups, and special programs. Five years later he was coordinating Prison Fellowship ministry outreach at four Massachusetts correctional institutions and was chosen as the PF National Volunteer of the Year.

After he retired, Dick organized one-day furloughs for inmates to perform community service work at a Christian camp and a housing complex for senior citizens. He rallied other church members including his pastor, who had never been in a prison before but who embraced prison ministry.

Bert and Dick represent the thousands of volunteers who go into correctional institutions every year under the Prison Fellowship banner to share the love of Christ. But there are many more who help deliver essential ministry services without ever setting foot inside a prison.

[CHAPTER 9]
On the Outside

By the mid-1980s more than twenty thousand volunteers were helping offenders, victims, their families, and the prison system look for answers through Prison Fellowship. By 1991, the number had doubled. To organize and coordinate them, Prison Fellowship set up Ministry Delivery Teams, community groups of Christians who assessed the local needs and worked with neighborhood churches to meet them.

Then and now, volunteers represent every component of America's melting-pot culture. A random sampling of Bible study leaders and Christian mentors might include a Mennonite grandmother in her lace cap, a college student in khakis and a T-shirt, a businesswoman in a suit and heels, and a college professor in tweeds and sensible shoes.

By their nature, in-prison seminars require volunteers to spend time behind bars themselves. But many others have donated their time and talents to prison ministry without ever going near a correctional institution; some of PF's most faithful supporters have never seen one. Either physical limitations, lack of opportunity, or personal preference have kept them on the outside. Yet these men and women are an essential part of the fabric of Prison Fellowship, enriching and strengthening it.

One of the most memorable and inspiring outside volunteers was Myrtie Howell. Myrtie married when she was seventeen years old. The year she turned forty-nine, her world fell apart—her father-in-law died, her mother died, and her husband was killed in a car wreck. Soon afterward, she lost her home. "I felt like Job," she admitted. "But it only made me lean closer on Christ."

Picking up the pieces, she got a job, then at the end of her working years moved to a small apartment in a retirement home. There she said the Lord directed her to write to prisoners. Not knowing where to write, she addressed a letter simply to "Atlanta Penitentiary, Atlanta," and offered to write to a prisoner there. Eventually the prison chaplain got the letter and told the inmates about Myrtie's offer. Before long Myrtie Howell had eight pen pals in the Atlanta prison and said she had "never been happier."

Myrtie began her prison ministry on her own. Prison Fellowship heard about her after an inmate wrote Chuck Colson asking him to pray for "Grandma Howell," because she was sick and "nobody has ever loved me like she has." PF started supplying Myrtie with names of new correspondents whenever she needed them. Featured in several *Jubilee* articles over the years, she put an endearing face on the pen pal ministry. She wrote faithfully until she died in 1986 at the age of ninety-six.

The Pen Pal Program was one of the earliest Prison Fellowship ministries and has given many prisoners their first connection with PF. When Fred Rhodes, then president of Prison Fellowship, started the *Jubilee* newsletter in the spring of 1977 there was a clip-out coupon on the back page inviting readers to volunteer to minister to prisoners; one option was by writing letters. The Pen Pal Program was a good way for a young ministry to extend its reach. There was no curriculum to pay for, no teacher training to plan, no capital expense, only a PF staff member or two to match up inmates with volunteer correspondents.

In the crowded and never-private world of prison, inmates are some of the most emotionally isolated people in the world, each man on a spiritual desert island. Prisoners often talk about being "ready to explode" because they can't confide in anyone, dream with anyone, console or be consoled. Behind the coarse language and bravado are desperately lonely human beings.

Most prisoners rarely have a visitor. Some are incarcerated far from their families; even those with friends and relatives close by find that the visits taper off after a few years. Their only remaining contact with the outside world—their only chance for spiritual and emotional release—is often through letters.

The Pen Pal Program was an immediate success. Today more than twelve thousand volunteers write regularly to seventeen thousand prisoners, with some volunteers writing three or four prisoners a week. Even so, PF maintains a steady backlog of a thousand prisoners looking for correspondents.

Pen pal friendships range from casual short-term exchanges to life-changing bonding experiences. A letter James Allison wrote in 1983 marked the beginning of one of the most intensely spiritual chapters in his life. Watching the TV news one night, Allison, a retired California school principal, was shocked and saddened to see his former student Jimmy Wingo had been arrested. Wingo escaped from a Los Angeles jail, where he was locked up for public drunkenness and petty theft. That same night, a man and his wife were killed nearby. Wingo was re-arrested and charged with two counts of murder. The trial lasted one day. Jimmy was convicted and sentenced to die in the electric chair.

Allison shared the news with a Prison Fellowship pen pal he already had, who suggested he write Jimmy too. Jimmy answered his letter, and the two wrote back and forth for months. Allison was moved enough by the friendship to visit Jimmy in prison and to meet Jimmy's mother and three of his children who lived nearby. Allison volunteered to lead a Prison Fellowship death row seminar there, which Jimmy enthusiastically attended.

As the execution date drew closer, the bond Jimmy and James first forged on paper grew as their shared love for Christ deepened. Others fought in the courts on Jimmy's behalf, convinced he was not guilty. In August 1986, they said prayers of thanksgiving at the news that Jimmy's execution was postponed. One man who believed Wingo was innocent was Jim McCloskey, a minister who appealed convictions he believed were unjust. McCloskey did all he could to win another stay of execution, but his second request was denied.

On Sunday, June 14, 1987, Jimmy's mother, three of his four children, and James Allison gathered around a table in the death house. James read from Exodus, where Moses turned bitter water sweet:

> Then Moses led Israel from the Red Sea and . . . three days they traveled in the desert without finding water. When they came to Marah, they could not drink its water becasue it was bitter; . . . So the people grumbled against Moses, saying, "What are we to drink?" Then Moses cried out to the LORD, and the LORD showed him a piece of wood. He threw it into the water, and the water became sweet. (Exod. 15:22–25 NASB)

Jimmy explained to his children that they had a right to be angry, but they mustn't seek revenge or be bitter. He told them to study the Bible and do their best to live by the teachings of Jesus. In his closing statement to the press, Jimmy forgave all who helped put him in the chair and all who were glad to see it.

James gave up his seat at the execution to Jim McCloskey, who "wanted to watch an innocent man die in the electric chair." Up to the moment Jimmy was led away to the execution chamber, James sat on a chair in the death house and held hands with him through the bars. Jimmy's final letter came later: "I suppose a lot of my peace is because after death I know I will be totally free. For death is but a stepping stone into eternal life for the Christian. One day, though, you will see me again in heaven, and when you get there, I will have a big bear hug waiting for you and proudly show you around."

The story of James and Jimmy shows how a simple letter can change the world for people at both ends of the postal route. Another transforming experience for volunteers and prisoners alike is giving a prisoner the chance to make restitution for his crime. For more than fifteen years, Prison Fellowship Community Service Projects have given inmates that chance, with opportunities to help build up communities rather than take from them, and to help reshape public perceptions about prisoners.

Community Service Projects (CSP) was born in a Virginia Beach coffee shop in 1981. Prison Fellowship vice president Ralph Veerman had just attended a program with Bob Moffat, cofounder of the National Association of Volunteers in Criminal Justice. The two talked about how important it was to encourage church members to go beyond donating money to ministry and get personally involved. They agreed there was no substitute for hands-on experience in understanding how Christian service really worked and in building up enthusiasm for service projects. The lesson was even more meaningful to Christian prisoners, who had little chance to contribute to the community.

By the time they left the table, Veerman and Moffat had the germ of an idea to furlough prisoners to work on community redevelopment projects in the Dominican Republic, where Moffat's ministry was well-established. Veerman suggested to target inmates from Elgin Federal Prison in Florida, which was relatively close to the Caribbean island nation.

Veerman excitedly presented his plan to federal prison chief Norm Carlson. While he remained one of PF's biggest supporters in Washington, Carlson believed furloughing prisoners outside the United States was impractical. Looking for an alternative, Ralph contacted his friend Bob Lupton of FCS Urban Ministries in Atlanta, who was also a volunteer PF seminar instructor. When Bob told him of a local service project in the works that the inmates could pitch in on, Norm Carlson approved furloughs for six prisoners, two whites, two blacks, and two Hispanics.

Describing the purpose of Community Service Projects, Chuck Colson explained they were to offer Christian inmates an opportunity to give of themselves in a meaningful way to those less fortunate.

> It will give inmates an opportunity to make restitution to the community that sent them to prison in the first place. . . . Too often prisoners are caught up in a very destructive cycle of self pity, and by being involved in caring for others, it takes their eyes off themselves and gives them a much more healthy perspective on their own incarceration.

The six inmates spent two weeks with church volunteers insulating the homes of Atlanta's poor, including two elderly widows. One of the ladies, Roxie Vaughn, was eighty-three years old, blind since birth, and lived alone in a tumbledown bungalow. With materials donated by local businesses, the men installed insulation, plastic storm windows and weather stripping, and caulked around drafty gaps and openings.

Every day after work, each inmate went home with a volunteer family. Other volunteers drove them back and forth and took care of the cooking. Even more than the work experience, these evenings spent in Christian homes made deep impressions on the prisoners. Most of them had little exposure to a safe and encouraging home environment. Seeing the possibilities was a boost to their spiritual lives that strengthened their own Christian walk and their witness when they returned to prison.

Response to the CSP was overwhelmingly positive. Prison Fellowship state directors coordinated available projects, sponsoring churches, and volunteers with prison chaplains and wardens who helped choose the participants. For two years beginning in 1984, Prison Fellowship also partnered with Habitat for Humanity to build houses for low-income families. Former President Jimmy Carter, a selfless spokesman and supporter of Habitat, and Chuck Colson worked together at one construction site.

Some of the people CSP helped already had a connection with Prison Fellowship. Frances Hart was thrilled to hear Prison Fellowship was helping refurbish her rotting three-room home in a Richmond neighborhood. One of her daughters was in prison, and Frances was caring for the daughter's two sons. She already knew of PF, and when she learned that a group of convicts was going to rebuild her house for free, she clapped her hands in an impromptu celebration and cried, "Oh my Lord! Thank you! Thank you!"

Details of the program changed as local conditions required. Sometimes men from the sponsoring churches hammered and sawed alongside the inmates; other times it was youth groups doing the work. Usually the inmates lived with volunteer host families for the two weeks they were furloughed, though sometimes they bunked at the church. Some projects were small, involving only one or two churches, while others saw nearly a hundred volunteers from several churches and local merchants donating materials worth tens of thousands of dollars.

CSP was extremely popular with community leaders and church groups. Church project coordinators praised it as the kind of ministry they'd been looking for to reach out to the community, eagerly recruiting volunteers to host furloughed participants. Leaders conducted special information sessions for volunteers emphasizing a few hard-and-fast rules, such as to not serve prisoners alcohol or let them drive. Still, even after the sessions, families scarcely knew what to expect; most of them had never seen a prisoner up close, much less ever invited one in for the night. A common presumption of many volunteers was that they were there to bless the prisoners, but when it was over they were the ones who felt blessed.

Hosts found they delighted in sharing everyday family experiences with the inmates—trips to the YMCA, Bible studies, watching videos, taking walks, doing garden work, and enjoying lively conversation around the dinner table. It got host families out of their comfort zones. One volunteer said, "God convicted me that I stereotype prisoners. I think the Lord was telling me, 'You're a sinner too.'"

One prisoner at the end of a CSP spoke for many when he said, "I thank God for this project, because it gave me an opportunity to draw closer to Him. I never thought anything positive would come out of me being in prison, but it has."

Another prisoner added, "You really don't know how other people will treat you when you get out. This project has shown me that there are a lot of good people out there. I felt a lot of love, and the Spirit of God."

An inmate participant in Iowa commented, "My entire Christian life has been behind bars, where other people have always come to me. The opportunity to give to someone else in this way has meant more to me than I can express adequately."

Keith, a fellow prisoner, agreed. "After all these years, to be able to do something for someone else instead of being taken care of is rewarding beyond measure."

One ecstatic homeowner, Ethel Gibson, simply but eloquently summed up the ministry: "There's Christians in every prison. The Lord sent them here. He knows where His children are. He has work for His children to do."

Eventually, Community Service Projects became a victim of its own success. The hours PF field staff and volunteers spent answering requests for projects from churches and community groups, furloughing prisoners, handling media relations, organizing volunteers, and so forth, began to overwhelm their ability to minister effectively. Even so, CSP served the ministry well at an important period in its growth. As Prison Fellowship matured, and as it continued fine-tuning its programs to reach the most people as effectively as possible, CSP was gradually phased out. It was one of a number of programs Prison Fellowship launched and curtailed over the years as needs, priorities, and resources changed.

One priority that has remained constant since the earliest days has been a commitment to helping prisoners readjust to life on the outside as well as helping them survive on the inside. Many ex-cons end up back in prison because while they're out, they see no choice but to go back to old habits. Looking for ways to improve an early support program for newly freed prisoners that helped them find a job and a place to live, PF inaugurated Philemon Fellowships in 1985.

The name comes from a book in the Bible. Paul wrote to Philemon from his prison cell asking him to welcome back a disobedient runaway named Onesimus, who had become a Christian under Paul's teaching. He wanted to make sure his young "son" in Christ got the chance to contribute to other lives, despite his earlier disobedience.

Philemon Fellowships are groups of recently released ex-offenders who meet once or twice a week with a volunteer leader to hold each other accountable, encourage each other, share their personal successes and disappointments, and exchange tips for making it on the outside. There's also Bible study, music, and refreshments afterward. It's a combination of a Christian refuge and an ex-offender networking center. To join, members have to have their parole officer's permission, have a church affiliation, make a one-year commitment, and agree to the Prison Fellowship Statement of Faith. If convicted of a new crime, they forfeit their membership.

Roger and JoAnn Ralston started a Philemon Fellowship in 1989 as a weekly discussion group for newly released prisoners in northern California. One early participant, Susie Pierce, praised the group for helping her "meet new, clean people and build bonds with people other than drug addicts." Local authorities agreed to support the fellowship; they referred ex-cons to the group.

The men originally met Friday afternoons, since that was when ex-prisoners were most tempted to veer back into their old lifestyles. Members later requested a second weekly meeting for in-depth Bible study. Philemon Fellowship members also raised money for prisoners' families and taught an alcohol recovery program to troubled kids in group homes. One member who spoke about alcohol abuse said, "I think they'll listen to us before they would listen to a lot of other people. We can tell them where they can end up, because we lived it all the way through."

Another member admitted, "All those years I used to hate everybody. The Lord just turns our hearts around—takes out them stony hearts and gives us pure hearts. I wanted to do something for the community, because for so long I tore it down."

Besides ministry groups, PF volunteers also mentor ex-prisoners individually through a variety of programs. It can be a time-consuming and emotionally exhausting commitment. But God steadily raises up men like Marcial Felan for the work. His friend, Victor Lopez, will be the first to declare that Marcial kept him out of prison and very probably saved his life.

Living in a penthouse suite with his wife and children, Victor looked back on a wild ride through the deadly world of Mexican drug smuggling and knew he'd beaten the system. Only a few years before he'd been a U.S. customs officer at the Mexican border in southern California, winning commendations for undercover work. Though he was an outstanding employee, his salary barely covered his family's expenses, much less his alcohol and cocaine addictions. When a man in a bar asked him to look the other way any time a certain car came to the border crossing, Victor told him it would cost five thousand dollars.

Soon he was looking the other way often enough to be a very wealthy man. He spent hundreds of dollars a night on dinner and champagne and showered his wife with jewelry and expensive cars. His mistress had access to a briefcase he kept filled with cash. "I thought I was cool," he recalled. "I had it all under control."

His confidence disappeared after a group of drug lords invited him and his family to breakfast. He thought at first he was moving into the big time. But in the dead of night before the scheduled meeting, the phone rang with an urgent message: he was being set up for a gangland execution. The bosses thought he had stolen forty tons of marijuana.

Victor hid in a safe house for two weeks while a cousin negotiated for his life. "I sweated a lot," Victor now admits. "I suddenly realized what I'd gotten myself into—what I'd gotten my family into."

The cousin made a deal and spared Victor's life. But then he found out that the U.S. government was looking for him too. He moved to Mexico and opened a restaurant. Flush with money and running a successful business, he moved into a penthouse and reveled in a life of luxury. Yet he couldn't stay away from the excitement of smuggling for long. Crossing the border with a supply of drugs, Victor was caught and arrested.

While Victor was out on bail, his wife became a Christian and asked him to spend a few minutes with her pastor, himself an ex-prisoner and recovering drug addict. The two men talked for eight hours. By the time the pastor rose to leave, Victor was a Christian too.

Guided by his newfound worldview, Victor pled guilty to the smuggling charges and received a sentence of four years hard time. He used the first year to read the Bible—and to quit drugs and alcohol cold turkey. Later he was transferred to prison in Big Spring, Texas, where, he said, "there were many Christians. We all got together for morning prayer and Bible studies," including Prison Fellowship lessons.

Life on the outside was hard for Victor after his release in 2000. His marriage fell apart and all his money was either confiscated or spent on legal fees. It would have been tempting to go back to old habits if it hadn't been for Marcial Felan, Prison Fellowship's local area director in San Diego. Another PF staffer, Roger Partain, strongly encouraged Victor to call Marcial when he got out, "because without a mentor," Partain warned, "you're not going to make it."

Victor took Roger's advice and learned a valuable lesson in waiting on the Lord's timing. Victor explained, "Marcial prayed. I'd call him up and he'd say, 'Let's pray.' We'd get together and we'd pray again. Finally I said, 'I'm forty-two years old and I don't have a job. I don't have a car. I don't have a place to live. And all you keep saying is pray.' Marcial said, "That's right. The Lord will take care of all that.'"

In time Victor landed a job with a detox program. "The Lord seemed to tell me, "This is the harm you did by bringing those drugs into the country; now you help clean it up!'" He also reconnected with his old friends in the U.S. Customs Service, who now use a video of Victor's experience in their training.

"I don't need the penthouses, the parties, and the Mercedes anymore," said this owner of a well-worn Pontiac. "All I need is to have peace in my life. And with Christ, that's what I have."

Of all the stories of Prison Fellowship volunteers assisting prisoners and their families on the outside, none has the scope and scale of the one that started with a soft-spoken woman from Alabama who carried a very nice shotgun.

CHAPTER 10

Remembering the Angels

At the same time film crews were busy shooting *Born Again* in 1978, a well-spoken and immaculately tailored woman walked out of state prison after six years behind bars. Her experience there led ultimately to the most popular and widely recognized single mission outreach in Prison Fellowship history. Breaking into a radiant smile during a video interview, she admitted, "Over the next five years a story unfolded that I wouldn't have believed if it wasn't my own."

Mary Kay Beard grew up rabbit hunting with her brothers. By the time she was grown, she was an expert shot with everything from a .22 to a .357 magnum. She married her husband nine days after they met on a blind date, then found out he was one of the most notorious safe-crackers in the United States. He quickly taught his new wife the tricks of the trade, and she used her own marksmanship skills to help out in the family business. "I was known as the Bonnie Parker of Alabama," she said, referring to the notorious gun-toting outlaw pair Bonnie Parker and Clyde Barrow. "My favorite was a sawed-off double-barrel shotgun in an attractive attaché case."

During their five years of marriage Mary Kay and her husband had everything they wanted. Then her world fell apart. Her husband left her, and she was captured and convicted of eleven federal and thirty-five state crimes including grand larceny and armed robbery. Her prison sentence, which could have been 180 years, was 21 years and a day. "When I was arrested I thought my life was over. But God was about to step in."

Mary Kay spent her first Christmas behind bars in 1972. Seeing a Christmas tree in the cellblock, she assumed the presents under it were little gifts the staff had bought for each other. Later she was surprised to learn that the bright packages were for prisoners.

"Between Thanksgiving and Christmas," Mary Kay explained, "everybody on earth came into prison—church groups and civic organizations—to give the women little presents." Mary Kay noticed that inmates hoarded and traded supplies of toothpaste, shampoo, soap, and other similar gifts that came in, then divided their collections into small piles on their bunks. "They wrapped the piles into presents with whatever scraps of colored paper or cloth they could find. Then on the last visiting Sunday before Christmas, they gave these as Christmas gifts to their children."

Mary Kay continued, "On the surface you wouldn't think any child would be excited about getting a little bottle of shampoo for Christmas, or that any mother would want to give it. But in the heart of a child, love is what's important. The item is immaterial. Women inside prison don't feel any differently about their children than women outside."

During a stretch in solitary confinement, Mary Kay began reading the Bible. In that desolate place God spoke to her heart. After a period of reflection and prayer, she gave her life to Christ based on the promise in Ezekiel 36:26: "I will give you a new heart and put a new spirit in you; I will remove from you your heart of stone and give you a heart of flesh."

In prison she earned a college diploma with honors from Auburn. Following her parole and remarriage in 1978, responding to what

Christ had done in her life as a prisoner, she joined Prison Fellowship as area director for Alabama, recruiting volunteers, forging partnerships with local churches, and helping open up prisons to PF ministries.

One day after she spoke at a luncheon on prison reform, a listener came up to her and said that instead of being more lenient, society should "lock 'em up and throw away the key."

"But what about the children of those prisoners?" Mary Kay asked.

The listener thought a minute, then told Mary Kay about how a local mall encouraged shoppers to buy something for poor children. Could the same thing work for children of prisoners?

Remembering the mothers who had been imprisoned with her, and what joy their modest Christmas gifts brought to the children, Mary Kay gathered a group of volunteers in the fall of 1982 and went into action. They collected the names of inmates' children from the chaplain at the prison where Mark Kay had served her time. Then they made construction paper angels for them all. Each angel had the name, age, and gender of a child. Mall managers in Montgomery and Birmingham let them set up trees the day after Thanksgiving and decorate them with the angels. Shoppers could select an angel, buy presents for that child, then bring them to a drop-off point. One key feature was that the presents would be given in the name of the incarcerated parent, not of the donor. Mary Kay called the program Christmas Angels.

In six days all the angels were taken and offers to buy presents still poured in; Mary Kay hurried back to the chaplain for more names. And so on Christmas Day 1982, 556 children unexpectedly received gifts from their incarcerated mothers, delivered to their homes by volunteers.

The program was an instant success. It raised awareness of the needs of children with imprisoned parents; it brought volunteers to Prison Fellowship who might not have been willing to go into a prison but wanted to do something; it strengthened the strained ties between prisoners and their families—ties that are crucial to an ex-offender's rehabilitation after release; it made a dramatic impact on other Prison

Fellowship ministries. In-prison Bible study attendance shot up. Hearing of a PF-sponsored event, inmates would ask, "Is this the group that bought Christmas gifts for my kids?"

The next Christmas more than twelve hundred children in ten cities received presents from their incarcerated parents thanks to Prison Fellowship. In ten years the number would grow to more than 260,000. By the year 2000, the ministry served more than 500,000 children a year; in 2005, more than 550,000.

Of the many changes and improvements in the ministry, over time, one of the first was renaming it Angel Tree. Also early on, Prison Fellowship decided to set up the trees in churches instead of malls. This change sparked lively debate among PF leadership. Some believed they should leave the trees in malls, since that's where the shoppers were and the program was so popular. Others insisted that Angel Tree was a Christian ministry and should be carried out through the churches. Finally they agreed to shift to the churches, confident that God would bless their efforts if He wanted them to continue.

As the Angel Tree list grew and more children received presents, organizers used several different methods to distribute them. Though volunteers usually wrapped the packages, PF also got permission to have wrapping sessions in prisons for parents, with corrections officers pitching in to help as well. Sometimes prisons even allowed Angel Tree celebrations in the facilities so the parents could give the presents in person. Some sponsoring churches hosted Angel Tree parties. In other places, volunteers delivered packages to the children's homes.

However it worked, the exchange made a memorable experience for the volunteers too. George Franklin got involved because he knew firsthand what it was like to be a parent in prison. "My main motivation was that I was incarcerated and didn't have the funds to buy my ten-year-old son presents. I never felt so useless in all my life. I started Angel Tree in Charlotte [NC] by getting churches involved. Regardless of what people feel about inmates, this is for the children. And it's a hands-on ministry, not an anonymous giveaway."

Dorcas Wilkinson, who coordinated Angel Tree for El Paso, Texas, exclaimed, "This is my Christmas! I get so involved and have talked to so many people—the children's guardians and wonderful church people. An inmate told us last year that Christmas is so lonely: you just sit there and think about home. But he said it made a difference to know his son would be opening a gift from him."

In communities where PF delivered presents to children at home, the volunteers saw everything from bright, clean middle-class houses to dark, dirty apartments, where various members of an extended family crowded together living off odd jobs and welfare checks. The hallways smelled of stale food and overwhelmed bathrooms. But the spirit of Christmas transformed even the most hopeless surroundings, especially when these unexpected strangers brought presents and Christmas greetings from a mother or father in prison.

While Angel Tree serves up a taste of Christmas spirit, it also helps reconcile families broken by a criminal conviction and the wrong choices leading up to it. A prisoner signing his children up for Angel Tree wrote, "Thank you very much for your help. You made my kids very happy and proud of me last Christmas. Please tell my kids I love them." Receiving a gift in another state, a child handed a note to a volunteer that read, "Would you please tell my daddy that I said thank you for the present and that I'm not mad at him anymore?"

As Mary Kay Beard remarked, "There is no government program, no fund that will buy them what their heart desires, but it is free to all who recognize the need. The only hope is in Jesus Christ."

At times Angel Tree has been the spark that brought an entire family to Christ. Mayra Abreu knew drugs were destroying her family and life was spiraling out of control. But she felt like there was nothing she could do. Her husband, Jose, had been in prison since last year for burglaries he committed to pay for his drug habit. She was addicted to crack cocaine and spent three years shuffling between homeless shelters and welfare hotels with her three children, Mencia, Alejandro, and Enriquillo.

Living in a Queens, New York, housing project, Mayra and her family went to sleep to the sounds of gunfire and voices of friends and strangers alike coming through day and night to buy drugs. When seven-year-old Mencia begged her mother to stop using drugs because they were devastating her fragile family, Mayra always promised she would but never followed through. "I was afraid for my mother," Mencia said, "that she would be dead somewhere." And she still missed her father, who had been transferred to a psychiatric institution for the criminally insane. "It's hard not to have a father," she said. "I believed in him so much. Even when he was in prison I loved him the same."

What seemed a hopeless situation set the scene for a remarkable recovery. A Christian volunteer in the psychiatric hospital introduced Jose to Christ. Eventually Jose gave his life to Him. Transferred back to the general prison population, Jose studiously attended Prison Fellowship seminars and Bible studies. With all the fire and passion of a new convert, he sent his wife Christian tracts and Bibles, and even arranged to have prison volunteers visit Mayra at home. But it was all too much. "Unfortunately, I got real pushy about it," Jose recalled. The harder he pushed, the more adamantly Mayra rejected Christianity.

In the fall of 1989, Jose signed up his children for Angel Tree gifts. He filled out forms all the time for this and that in prison, and Angel Tree was nothing more than a vague promise that somebody was supposed to do something for his kids at Christmas. He didn't have any grand expectations that it would come to anything.

On Christmas Eve, Mayra answered a knock at her dingy public housing apartment to find "a UPS guy with a *big* box!" Inside a card said "From Jose Abreu." How could Jose buy anything? He was in prison. Then she remembered he had told her something about Angel Tree. Her eyes welled up with tears as she recalled, "My kids were crying and jumping up and down and hugging me saying, 'Mommie! Look what I have!'"

There was a toy for each of the children and clothes for everyone. "That is when I cried out to God, and I knew that He loved me," said Mayra. "I accepted the Lord Jesus Christ into my life. And then I prayed with my kids that God would help me stop this bad habit, to take this drug addiction away from me, so I can be the mom they deserve."

That night both Mayra and Mencia gave their lives to Christ. And Mayra never took drugs again.

In 1990 Jose got out of prison and, he said, "I brought Jesus with me." He and his wife both got steady jobs and volunteered for their church's prison ministry. They never found out who bought the Angel Tree presents that so dramatically redirected their lives. But to them those anonymous packages were "a gift from heaven."

Ten years later Jose and Mayra both were involved with Prison Fellowship in New York, Jose leading in-prison seminars and Mayra working with Angel Tree ministry. They were serving as foster parents to three children who were born in prison. They had enough room for the additions because they moved to a four-bedroom house that they helped overhaul through Habitat for Humanity, working six hundred hours for their down payment. For the first time ever, there was a fenced yard for the children to play in.

God had greatly blessed them, but He also had more mountains for them to climb. In 2000, Mayra donated part of her liver so Jose could have a transplant to replace his organ destroyed by years of alcohol and drug abuse. Drug reactions and other problems stretched out his recovery to more than two years.

That crisis was scarcely past when the U.S. Immigration Service notified Jose that he might be deported for his past acts of moral turpitude. Chuck Colson and other Prison Fellowship leaders rallied to his defense and gave compelling evidence of his transformed life. Waiting to learn the outcome of his hearing, Jose said confidently, "God is the One who takes care of me. I rely on the Lord."

Angel Tree Camping, which began in 2001, reaches out to children of prisoners in the summer, matching kids with local churches that can send them to camp. Home life for these children, particularly in the inner city, is hard year-round, not just at Christmas. Most inner-city kids are surrounded by negative influences and have no positive role models or spiritual guidance. Research by the Barna Group shows that a person is five times more likely to come to Christ between ages five and thirteen than any other time. Christian summer camp is an ideal place to reveal the gospel to children when they're most likely to be interested in it.

Angel Tree Camping, established with a generous gift from Rick and Helen DeVos, makes referrals to camps accredited by Christian Camping International and supplies churches with step-by-step guidelines on how the program works. PF gives a backpack and a Bible to every Angel Tree camper, and scholarships to those who need help with camping fees. Through the generosity of Prison Fellowship donors, the ministry pays more than one million dollars in scholarships each summer to help some ten thousand children.

The ministry gives many young campers from the city their first look at a forest, first swim in a lake, first ride on horseback, and first experience surrounded by attentive, caring, Christian adults. They have a chance to read the Bible and learn about their Creator while surrounded by the beauty of His creation. Some campers come back year after year, strengthening the effect of Christian influences on them and on their families back home. And when they're at camp, they aren't on the street picking up bad habits.

In 2004 Angel Tree sprouted yet another branch, Angel Tree Mentoring. Whereas the camping program added a summer vacation balance to

Angel Tree's traditional Christmas ministry, Angel Tree Mentoring responded to a child's year-round need for guidance and affirmation. The general decline in traditional moral values since the 1960s has made it harder than ever for children to come to Christ and uphold His values in their daily lives. Furthermore, the message is in constant danger of being muddled. The Barna Group reported that only 9 percent of born-again teenagers believe in moral absolutes.

Angel Tree Mentoring is a program that matches a prisoner's child with an adult Christian mentor willing to invest for the long term in sharing the gospel, building young disciples, and multiplying laborers for God's harvest.

In 2003 Prison Fellowship published *Six Million Angels*, a collection of stories from some of the six million children served by Angel Tree over the previous twenty years. Time and again presents at Christmas served to renew relationships that had been shattered, sometimes for many years, by a prison sentence.

Boyd hadn't spoken with his ex-wife or nine-year-old son in almost three years. Disgusted with his repeated lies and broken promises, she had cut off all contact even after he wrote that he had become a new man in Jesus Christ. In 1994 he signed his son up for Angel Tree and resigned himself to getting through the holidays without hearing from them.

He was amazed, then, during a Christmas Day phone conversation with his father, to hear that his ex-wife wanted him to call her. When he got her on the line, she was giddy with excitement about the presents their son had received from him: a sweater, a basketball, a children's Bible with his name on it, and a tie "to wear to church." Then Boyd got a Christmas present of his own that absolutely astonished him. She said, "Would you add our names to the prison visiting list? We want to come and visit"—all the way from Ohio to Florida.

His heart pounded as she handed the phone to their son, Drew. For the first time ever, he asked Drew to forgive him for all the suffering he'd caused the family. Drew answered, "I love you, Dad. I think about you every day."

Summing up his thoughts in a letter to Prison Fellowship, Boyd said, "God over-answered my prayers. I just had to let you know that God is using your ministry. God bless you all!"

One of Chuck Colson's favorite Angel Tree stories took place in Oregon the week before Christmas 1996. The pastor of a small church there was putting the finishing touches on his sermon when he heard a faint knock. Opening the door he saw three disheveled children: boys aged five and three and their two-year-old sister. They'd received Angel Tree gifts from the church. Their father was in prison and their mother was caught up in drugs and prostitution.

"Mister, can we see the church that bought us all those Christmas presents?" the oldest asked.

"Of course you can. Come on," the pastor replied, and took them on a tour of the small church. The children thanked him and left, and he returned to his work.

A few minutes later there was another knock. The children were back. "What time does church start?" the five-year-old wanted to know.

"In an hour," the pastor said.

"We'll be back."

Fifteen minutes later there was another knock.

"Is it okay for a person to come to church if his socks don't match?"

"Of course!"

"Is it okay to come if you don't have socks at all?"

"Sure. Why?"

"Because my socks don't match, and my little brother doesn't have any socks at all."

"You come just as you are," said the pastor, sweeping the children into the sanctuary and seating them with a kindly couple. During the service the couple noticed the older boy had a paper sack with him.

"What's in your bag?" the man asked quietly.

"We didn't know how long the service would be, so we brought our lunch."

Inside was a single hot dog the three planned to split.

From that day on, the trio of youngsters became a part of the congregation. It was a case, Chuck explained, where Angel Tree "literally opened the door to a church [these children] would never have dreamed of approaching on their own. This story is a powerful metaphor for the church at large. Jesus didn't tell us to sit and wait for the world to come to us. He says, 'Go and make disciples.'"

Shirley DeLoach was a Prison Fellowship area director who took Jesus's instructions to heart. In 1993 she received an Angel Tree request from Marianne Bullock, whose two children lived with their grandmother half a continent away in Washington State. Marianne had recently come to Christ following a PF in-prison seminar, but only after a short, wild, and tragic life. At twenty-seven, the former drug addict and prostitute was dying of AIDS.

Later in the year Marianne's adoptive mother, who learned of Prison Fellowship through the Angel Tree connection, called the ministry in Washington and asked if they could have someone visit Marianne in Louisiana on her family's behalf before she died.

Shirley agreed to make the visit herself and visited Marianne in the prison infirmary the next day. Clearly her time was growing short. From her bed she rasped out a desperate request. "Can you help me not to die in prison?"

Shirley jumped fearlessly into the sea of red tape separating Marianne from her family. She worked local, state, and national connections including social services and the Department of Corrections. Because Marianne was a Blackfoot Indian, she also called in the Bureau of Indian Affairs. She found a Christian AIDS ministry to supply an air ambulance and a doctor, and nursing home in Washington willing to take Marianne's case. After two months of paperwork and the governor's signature, Marianne flew to Tacoma. She saw her children and died a week later in the care of her mother, surrounded by a host of Christian friends who gently helped her make a sad passage to a glorious eternity. The stories of Angel Tree are powerful and precious. Some tell of comfort in a time of loss, while others reflect a spirit of unbounded joy. The sheer number of them has had an impact for the ministry. Prisoners who have never heard of Prison Fellowship or Jesus Christ know all about Angel Tree. Without judgment or condemnation, it reaches into their world and gives them a chance to show they love their children.

While the program brightens prisoners' lives, it also plays an esential role in breaking the family cycle of crime. Children of convicts are two to three times more likely to be criminals than the average population. Knowing their incarcerated parent loves them, seeing a selfless alternative to criminal behavior through an Angel Tree volunteer, recognizing Christ in their lives—these transform not only children's Christmases, but also their futures.

[CHAPTER 11]
Crime and Justice

Prison Fellowship began as a ministry to encourage Christian prisoners in their faith and to give them the tools to share the gospel with others behind bars. It wasn't long though before Chuck Colson and his leadership team realized that to effectively reinforce or transform an inmate's spiritual life they had to do more than that. Helping inmates find God behind bars would never be fully effective in redirecting their lives as long as they were treated as unredeemable misfits in and out of prison, and as long as the culture they came from was so hostile to Christian principles.

With the prison population growing fifteen times faster than the general census, society was producing criminals quicker than in-prison Bible teaching could reform them. To stem the tide of new and repeat offenders, Prison Fellowship looked upstream from sentencing and incarceration to see why people became criminals in the first place and what Christian teaching could do about it. As PF continued developing and expanding its various ministry programs, it also began promoting judicial and cultural reform. Ministry dealt with the results of crime; reform addressed its causes. As Prison Fellowship matured, these goals—ministry and reform bearing the fruits of faith and justice—became its two prime objectives.

The first focus on reform came in October 1979, after Chuck visited the penitentiary at Walla Walla, Washington. "There," he later said, "I had an epiphany. I realized that you can't preach to prisoners without addressing justice." That day marked the point when Prison Fellowship began widening its mission field beyond the cellblock and the prison chapel, spilling over the walls and razor wire into the world inmates had come from and to which most of them would return. To reach offenders in the long term, Prison Fellowship would look more and more at transforming the worldview of the culture that nurtured them.

Built in 1886, the prison at Walla Walla was notorious for its "bucket cells" without toilet facilities or running water, where inmates used a bucket to answer the calls of nature. It was by Colson's reckoning "one of the worst prisons in America—overcrowded, filthy, and out of control." Walking through the gates, he felt a sense of foreboding and apprehension. He had been in a long list of prisons by this time and was sometimes nervous or ill at ease for one reason or another, but he never before thought that something catastrophic was about to happen. "I could smell the tension," he said.

Until the day before Chuck arrived, the prison had been locked down for four months following the murder of a guard; he was the first visitor allowed inside since the tragedy. Twelve hundred offenders were shut away in their cells twenty-three hours a day. Communication between the prisoners and staff had completely broken down. The inmate council had been disbanded, and the process for dealing with grievances short-circuited. Guards warned him not to go in because it was too dangerous, but Chuck explained he had promised to lead a Bible study.

Riot police stood by, as Colson went in and addressed a small gathering of about 150 men to explain about Prison Fellowship and share the gospel. "The reaction was stony silence," he said. But it was almost much worse than that.

The inmates, Colson later learned, had planned a riot for that day. Angry and desperate to be heard, they targeted five guards for death and decided to take Colson hostage. But after he spoke, Don, an inmate leader who had been a Christian only a few months, got up from his front row seat and asked, "Mr. Colson, why should we think you're real?"

Chuck answered, "What can I do for you?"

Don replied, "If you really mean what you say, don't leave us. We need hope. We need someone who cares about us. Go outside and tell the world what you see here."

"If I do that, what will you do?"

"I'll run your Bible study for you."

Working quickly behind the scenes after the speech was over, Don convinced his collaborators to cancel their planned riot because he believed they could trust Colson to present their grievances to the warden.

Outside the prison, Colson faced a crowd of reporters wanting the first news from the inside since the lockdown began. He told them it was intolerable to treat prisoners like animals in a cage and then expect them to come out rehabilitated and ready to start a new life. Colson began a dialogue with the prison administration, which continued under Prison Fellowship instructors George Soltau and Al Elliott for eighteen months. For most of that time, PF was the only channel of communication both sides trusted. Gradually, with George and Al as intermediaries, inmates and officials agreed on a new grievance procedure and reestablished the inmate council. Meanwhile Colson and others worked to pass legislation in Washington State; Chuck's description of the deplorable conditions at Walla Walla led to what he characterized as "desperately needed reforms."

The experience marked a major step for Prison Fellowship beyond prison evangelism toward political action. "No one stopped to ask whether prison conditions were our proper concern," Colson wrote in *Jubilee*.

We are ministers of the gospel message, to be sure; but to tell a group of angry inmates that we are interested only in preaching a spiritual message and not with their actual conditions—then literally a matter of life and death—would have been unthinkable. . . . It is simply not possible to minister in prison without being concerned for inmates' welfare, and for basic principles of God's justice for all men. . . . There's no way to tell people about Jesus without exhibiting towards them the same love and concern that He did during His earthly ministry.

Prison Fellowship identified a strong correlation between the soaring prison population and what Chuck described as "society's moral breakdown." He added, "I have become convinced that meshing prison ministry with worldview teaching is God's providential plan for this ministry." PF eventually grew dramatically in that direction, though it was several years before it reached the level Colson envisioned.

One reason prisons had become such ghastly places was because courts had repeatedly denied prisoners access to the court system to complain about mistreatment or petition for improvements. That situation also began to change, as Lloyd C. Anderson reported in his book *Voices from a Southern Prison*, documenting the experience of a Kentucky inmate named Shorty Thompson.

Shorty had been in and out of prison for almost twenty years when he drew a five-year sentence in 1977 for helping a destitute friend steal and butcher two cows. He served at the Kentucky State Reformatory in LaGrange, near Louisville.

KSR was built in 1937 using the same kind of dormitory layout Chuck Colson lived in at Maxwell. The style had replaced cells beginning around 1900, after some prison officials decided that criminals couldn't actually change and that the goal of prison was not to rehabilitate, but to keep wrongdoers away from the law-abiding public. In Anderson's words, "Since there was little hope of reforming the prisoners, there was little need for individual cells, except for disciplinary confinement." Administrators called the dormitory-style facilities "warehouse prisons."

When Shorty arrived at KSR, there were more than two thousand inmates crowded into space designed for twelve hundred. He stood in line an hour for meals, half that time outside in all weather—rain, snow, subzero temperatures—with only a light prison-issued jacket for cover. Hot water was rare. There weren't enough sinks or toilets and most fixtures were broken anyway. Inmates punched holes in the sewer lines so the toilets would flush, spilling human waste under the buildings where it collected six inches deep.

More than all the crowding and filth, Shorty despised the rats and bugs that lived everywhere—in the walls and ceilings, in the sinks, in his sheets, in his pockets, and often in his food. Even a visiting judge had to pick a roach out of his pudding.

In the fall of 1978, Shorty wrote a one-page petition to the federal court in Louisville and convinced five other prisoners to sign it, even though the penalty for signing a petition at KSR was solitary confinement. When guards found out about the petition, they started harassing and threatening the six men, roughing them up, surrounding them, and holding shotguns to their heads; someone slipped marijuana into their mail.

Against all odds, Shorty's petition made it through the court system and prompted an investigation. Criminal psychologist Dr. Richard Korn reported that the "dilapidated, filthy, vermin-infested dormitories" at KSR were dangerously overcrowded. The result was "[c]onstant over-exposure and over-stimulation [leading] to bizarre and degrading forms of tension-release. Homosexuality, both consensual and coerced, is endemic, public, and inescapable even to non-participants who are forced to be spectators to noisy, night-long orgies in neighboring bunks."

In *Voices from a Southern Prison*, Lloyd C. Anderson summarized some of the other investigative findings, which closely paralleled Chuck Colson's observations and conclusions:

At best, KSR was doing very little to prepare the majority of prisoners for life in free society. At worst, the prison was instilling disrespect for work and destroying the men's motivation to improve themselves. . . . Inmates were locked in their wings from 6:00 p.m. to 6:00 a.m., so that for twelve hours fifty to sixty convicts were packed together, largely unsupervised, in space designed for thirty. The guard on duty often was called to the mess hall before 6:00 a.m. to help supervise breakfast. During these early morning hours the entire dormitory would have no guard at all. The result was that stronger prisoners committed massive amounts of crime against weaker prisoners, crimes that can never be detected or recorded: robbery, assault, homosexual rape. If a younger, weaker prisoner was afraid of being raped in his bunk, his solution at KSR was to find a "daddy," an older, stronger homosexual who would protect his charge against rape in return for sex wherever, whenever, and however he wanted it. . . . Weapons such as knives, pipes, and guns were readily available. . . . A prisoner could buy a sawed-off shotgun on the Yard in about fifteen minutes. It was easy to get drugs and alcohol. If a man wanted moonshine to help pass the time, for example, the only question was whether he wanted apple, strawberry, or some other flavor.

The State of Kentucky eventually paid a four million dollar fine and spent another two hundred million dollars on prison upgrades. Other states took notice and started giving more attention to the way their prisoners lived. Even so, improving prisons on a wide scale continued to be an uphill battle against a host of challenges: budget cuts, political timidity, inertia, prejudice, physical isolation, ignorance.

Looking at prisoners and listening to their stories, Chuck Colson kept returning to the question: What kind of society produces these people? Witnessing to them and preaching the gospel after they'd broken the law was an uphill battle. Yes, people could find Christ in prison, and even one soul saved was cause for rejoicing. But for every prisoner who became a Christian, two or three or ten took his place. The supply of lost and broken people was far outstripping the ability of Prison Fellowship or any other ministry to meet the need.

Returning to the Walla Walla prison in 1981, Colson was accompanied by a young attorney from Chicago named Daniel Van Ness, who had recently left his position with a church-sponsored law clinic to become special counsel on criminal justice to Prison Fellowship. Being burglarized himself made Dan realize that the criminal justice system he knew as a lawyer was completely detached from his experience as a victim. Van Ness made the initial presentation to the PF board for a ministry focused specifically on justice reform. "Instead of patching," he said, "let's change the criminal justice system. It may take a generation, but it's worth doing."

"It was a time," Colson later wrote, "when I first realized that we weren't going to do anything about the criminal justice problem, the exploding prison populations, until we did something about the breakdown of moral values in our culture." The board agreed, and in 1983 established Justice Fellowship with Van Ness as president. The new ministry would focus on the relationship between morality and crime.

Colson's position was underscored by research. *The Criminal Personality*, a study in the 1970s by Stanton Samenow and Samuel Yokelson, made the first compelling statistical ties between crime and morality. *Crime and Human Nature*, a later study by Harvard social scientists James Q. Wilson and Richard Hernstein, reinforced the connection between moral choices and criminal behavior. Colson said, "I began to see that we couldn't just preach in the prisons. We couldn't even just be concerned with systemic problems in the criminal justice system. We had to also deal with the moral collapse of the culture."

Justice Fellowship immediately began staking out positions on prison legislation. In 1983 Colson, PF board member and drugstore entrepreneur Jack Eckerd, state attorney general Jim Smith, and Judge Harry Fogle supported Florida prison reform bills which passed virtually unopposed. From an average increase of 366 prisoners a month, the new laws reduced the prison population by 2,000 in two years, relieving severe overcrowding.

An Indiana task force supported by Justice Fellowship got approval from its legislature to start restitution and community service projects with nonviolent offenders. Indiana state senator William Costas and chairman of Senate Judiciary Committee Edward Pease read the Justice Fellowship newsletter articles to the legislature and contacted JF for help promoting intensive supervision as opposed to imprisonment.

Nationally JF collaborated with Sam Nunn (D-GA) and William Armstrong (R-CA) to add a resolution to the federal Sentencing Improvement Act calling on judges to punish nonviolent offenders with restitution and community service. The act was passed, and signed by President Ronald Reagan October 1, 1984—the first national legislation influenced by Justice Fellowship.

Van Ness, and his lean staff of five, monitored state and national legislation for news of prison-related bills. When they identified a proposed law as one that would promote restitution and community service as alternatives to prison for nonviolent criminals, they formed task forces to influence state decisionmakers. By the end of 1985, Justice Fellowship was at work in fifteen states plus the District of Columbia.

Writing in the JF newsletter, "Justice Report," Van Ness explained, "The Bible teaches that criminals do more than break the law, they cause injury that needs tending, both to the victim and the community. JF calls it Restorative Justice." He made an example of VICTOR (Victim-Offender Reconciliation Program) in Columbia, South Carolina, which brought crime victims and nonviolent offenders together with a trained mediator to add biblical principles to the criminal justice system. These were steps in reversing centuries of legal precedent that assumed the state was the victim of a crime, rather than the actual victim. The idea was rooted in ancient England, where deer poachers were charged with a violation against the king.

Colson shared his thoughts on crime and morality in a speech to the National Religious Broadcasters during their 1985 convention. Talking about "worldview" in those days, Chuck recalled, "drew all kinds of blank stares." Historically prison ministry meant working through the chaplain's office to bring Christian programs to inmates. Going beyond that, and the rationale for doing so, were alien concepts then even to Christians in the business of broadcasting the gospel.

About the same time as his NRB appearance, Chuck started writing a column on the inside back cover of *Christianity Today* magazine. There, too, he explored the question of how the culture influenced criminal behavior, what America's choices were on the issue, and the consequence of those choices. Chuck coined the phrase "new barbarism" to describe the result of changing attitudes and values in society, "the relativism that has undermined any absolute standard of conduct, destroying a sense of duty, commitment, honor." In one of his monthly *Jubilee* columns he expanded on the topic:

> The family, ordained by God as the basic unit of human organization, is necessary not only for propagating the race, but as the first school of human instruction. . . . When the first school of instruction is fragmented and invaded by the barbaric, radical individualism of our age, moral values fall by the wayside. The result is people who know no higher law than their own appetites—young men and women with their moral sense sucked out of them. In such a vacuum of character, barbarism flourishes in a younger generation. The younger barbarians live not only in the long corridors of Rikers Island; they are overflowing the suburbs, spilling out of elegant country homes, lurking in exclusive private schools.

In 1986, Dan Van Ness wrote *Crime and Its Victims* to explore more fully the faults of a criminal justice system that neglects restitution and too often ignores the victim:

> For one brief moment, the victim and the offender confront each other. The crime establishes a relationship in which one wounds another. But we never deal with the wound. We try offenders when we catch them. And we sometimes send them to prison, not for the injury done to the victims, but because they broke the law. So now we have two wounds and no healing.
>
> The wounds multiply. Friends and neighbors of the victim, concerned for their own safety, start taking greater precautions. Fear is also a wound. The families of prisoners, unable to deal with the separation and stigma, begin to draw apart. Another wound. The victims who are reorganizing and the prisoners who are being released discover that the community cannot accept them as victims and ex-prisoners, and they conceal that part of themselves. More wounds.
>
> We must hold these offenders accountable. They have broken the law; they have hurt others. If we do not insist that those who commit crimes be held responsible for their actions, we begin a slide into anarchy. But the offender can be held responsible in many ways. It is in our best interest to find those ways that heal wounds, not create new ones.

By 1988 thirty-seven states were under court order to reduce prison crowding due in part to mandatory sentencing and other tough-on-crime measures. That year James Austin, director of research for the National Council on Crime and Delinquency, echoed JF's position when he said,

> We've got to look for something other than building new prisons. That won't make us safer. In California, we've tripled the prison population since 1977, but the crime rate hasn't changed one bit. Trying to solve the crime problem by building more prison cells is like trying to solve the problem of AIDS by building more hospitals.

Justice Fellowship continued to raise its profile in the public debate on crime. In 1989 Steve Varnam, an ex-offender and already a regional director of the ministry, became the first director of field operations, coordinating all the regional directors and ten standing state task forces, as well as organizing task forces in ten more states. May 12 of that year, *The Washington Post* published an editorial by Colson and Van Ness explaining four goals the ministry had developed:

1. Allowing victims to pursue civil damages as part of a criminal case
2. Sentencing nonviolent criminals to perform community-based restitution instead of being locked up (particularly timely in light of televangelist Jim Bakker's forty-five-year sentence that year for defrauding his contributors, compared to an average sentence of eighteen years for murder and eight and one-half years for rape)
3. Strengthening victim assistance programs, especially by getting churches more involved
4. Expanding victim/offender reconciliation programs

Encouraging stories in the press proved that prisoners could be productive members of society as well as active in their own rehabilitation. In 1989 Best Western hotels employed female inmates in Arizona as telephone reservation clerks. That year eighteen inmates earned more than one hundred thousand dollars and paid more than twenty thousand dollars in taxes and twenty-four thousand dollars in room and board. Such positive accounts help offset the opposition to prisoners working from some corrections officials, who thought it was too much trouble or too dangerous, and from some workers and employers who considered prisoners unfair competition.

Dan Van Ness resigned as president of Justice Fellowship in 1992 to earn a master of law degree from Georgetown Law Center in

Washington, remaining as part-time counsel. Colson praised his work, saying, "Dan's genius, and the key to JF's success, has been the ability to translate this abstract notion of justice into a specific, tangible plan for criminal justice reform." Steve Varnam took over leadership of the ministry as executive director. In 1993, in light of Prison Fellowship's growing interest in cultural and public policy issues, Justice Fellowship became its own full subsidiary with a separate board of directors and funding base. That year volunteer task forces in twenty-five states collaborated with legislators and criminal justice officials to promote correctional reforms based on biblical principles.

As sensible as the idea to operate Justice Fellowship independently seemed at the time, the new arrangement led to a struggle. Donors seemed more interested in supporting prison ministry than prison reform. While Prison Fellowship's income moved more or less steadily upward, Justice Fellowship had a hard time cultivating a donor base big enough to sustain operations. Prison ministry produced an endless stream of heartwarming stories of men, women, families, and volunteers whose lives were enriched by Prison Fellowship. These were personal victories donors could understand and relate to. Justice Fellowship, though ultimately its work also improved lives, was active more in the halls of state capitols, at community group meetings, and among the red tape of legislative procedure. Attracting contributors to that work proved a much tougher sell.

In 1996 Prison Fellowship restructured Justice Fellowship once again, installing Varnam as chief operating officer and reviving the title of president. An executive headhunter found a new president for Justice Fellowship in Spokane, Washington. Under other circumstances the candidate might have turned them down in anticipation of taking the rostrum as Speaker of the House of the California legislature. As it was, he was just completing twenty-five months in prison.

Pat Nolan had been a rising young star in California politics, almost certain to become the first Republican Speaker of the House in decades.

After that, he had his sights on the governor's chair. Everything changed when the FBI raided his office during a campaign finance investigation and charged him with racketeering. He was innocent, but he was targeted by political opponents who bribed one of his staff members to claim she had "delivered" his vote. Faced with a minimum eight-year sentence if convicted, he was offered a plea bargain that would reduce his sentence to twenty-five months. He and his wife considered the consequences of eight years' imprisonment on their three children, ages five years, four years, and ten months.

He said simply, "I agreed to plead guilty to something I hadn't done and did my time. It was obviously very tough. But it didn't make me bitter, because I went into prison believing in God, but I came out knowing Him."

As his release date approached, Nolan pondered what to do with his life. He'd had several lucrative job offers, but he wanted to move in a different direction. "I wanted to take what I learned inside prison and use it to improve the system." Because the noise and lack of privacy in prison made it hard to pray with focus and concentration, Pat often prayed while using the exercise equipment. One day he prayed particularly for God to guide him in making plans for the future. God seemed to answer, "I will take care of your family."

Coming back from lunch that day he heard the ominous command over the loudspeaker: "Pat Nolan, report to control!" The order to report usually meant an inmate had violated some rule and was in trouble. When he reported he saw "the meanest guard" in the whole complex waiting for him. He held out a note and said, "Nolan, you got a phone call."

Phone call? Prisoners weren't allowed to receive phone calls. The staff never took messages for inmates. Pat returned the call; it was a headhunter looking for a new president for Justice Fellowship. Was he interested? A half-hour earlier, God had promised, "I will take care of your family." Here that promise was being fulfilled. Members of the

Prison Fellowship board flew to Spokane to interview him in prison. Would he accept the position? "It fit every criteria I wanted for a job," Pat explained. "It allowed me to be with my family; it allowed me to serve the church; it allowed me to use my experiences in prison to help change the law, and it knitted together my training as a lawyer, my time in the legislature, and my time in prison. Any one of those not being there, I wouldn't be able to do this job. I said yes. So clearly was God in this I seriously would have been fearful of His wrath if I hadn't."

After two years as president of an independent Justice Fellowship, and two years of searching for sustained donor support, Pat oversaw the ministry's reintegration into the larger Prison Fellowship organization. But the ministry that welcomed JF back as a new division in 1998 was far different from the one that had set it in motion fourteen years before. Justice Fellowship became part of an unprecedented forum for defending the Christian worldview and underscoring its impact on the culture.

CHAPTER 12

Wilberforce Reformation

During the 1980s Prison Fellowship matured into a big-picture movement to reclaim the culture for Christianity. It wasn't that PF was abandoning its original purpose, but that in order to achieve it, it had to respond to the cultural influences that lead to criminal behavior. Commenting on the changing perspective in 1991 Colson said,

> We've never had a narrow vision of the ministry. The vision is to exhort and assist the church in its ministry to prisoners. But from the beginning it has also been to challenge the false values of the culture. PF stands for a witness of the kingdom of God being made visible in an area of desperate human need and failure.

Prison Fellowship first highlighted the issue of cultural influence in a series of ninety-second radio commentaries Chuck broadcast in 1979 titled *Another Point of View*. He returned to the medium ten years later, when a friend of the ministry offered to support two months of radio shows to see if it was a worthwhile communication tool. The result was a series of eight weekly half-hour programs called

Against the Night. A network of stations carried the show along with additional short daily commentaries, but Prison Fellowship never was sure how cost effective the experiment was.

Then in September 1991, Chuck began a series of short daily radio commentaries called *BreakPoint.* These concise audio essays delivered a concentrated dose of the Prison Fellowship worldview to a wider audience than ever before. Consistently and tirelessly, Colson re-affirmed the conviction that crime was at its heart a moral issue. Eventually more than a thousand stations carried *BreakPoint* to a potential audience of a million listeners every weekday. The immediacy and reach of this powerful medium gave the message exposure and wide impact outside prison policy and lawmaking circles. It provided a powerful way for PF to present and defend its worldview in the marketplace of ideas, reaching people who had no previous connection to prisoners or prison programs.

Together Justice Fellowship and *BreakPoint* anchored the PF drive to articulate and defend its Christian worldview. These became two of the foundational building blocks of a whole range of ministry programs named in honor of Colson's great hero of the faith, William Wilberforce. Colson came to appreciate Wilberforce during the process of studying great Christian thinkers and solidifying his own worldview, a process that began in the first years of his ministry.

It was 1978 when Colson first heard American minister and teacher Francis Schaeffer preaching on the theories of Abraham Kuyper at L'Abri, Schaeffer's Christian study center in Switzerland. Kuyper was a great educator, editor, and statesman who later became prime minister of the Netherlands. "It quickly challenged me to think about things in a broader context," Colson said.

Colson's friend D. James Kennedy, pastor of Coral Ridge Presbyterian Church in Ft. Lauderdale, also steered him toward Kuyper. "We had lunch at the invitation of one of his friends," Chuck explained. "Jim thought I was getting a little bit off the reservation theologically. He said, 'You have to promise me you'll read Abraham Kuyper's lectures [on the teachings of seventeenth-century French Protestant reformer John Calvin] given at Princeton in 1898.' So I did. And that along with my reading of Schaeffer was really life-changing. I began to develop a worldview."

Kuyper positioned Christianity in general, and the teachings of Calvin in particular, as a "life system" that went far beyond reading the Bible and going to church. Mankind was all one before God, he said, and therefore had no special authority over each other. "All men or women, rich or poor, weak or strong, dull or talented, as creatures of God, and as lost sinners, have no claim whatsoever to lord over one another. . . . We stand as equals before God, and consequently equal as man to man."

In his sixth and final lecture in the Princeton series, "Calvinism and the Future," Kuyper laid down a marker for Christians that Colson and his ministry picked up with fervor more than eighty years later. "Calvin's Christianity," Kuyper concluded, "did not stop at a church-order, but expanded in a life-system, and did not exhaust its energy in a dogmatical construction, but created a life- and worldview, and such a one as was, and still is, able to fit itself to the needs of every stage of human development, in every department of life."

Modernism now confronts Christianity; and against this deadly danger, ye, Christians, cannot successfully defend your sanctuary but by a life- and worldview of your own, founded as firmly on the base of your own principle, wrought out with the same clearness and glittering in an equally logical consistency. Now this is not obtained by either Christian works or mysticism, but only by going back, our hearts full of mystical warmth and our personal faith manifesting itself in abundant fruit, to that turning-point in history, and in the development of humanity which was reached in the Reformation [of Calvin's time]. . . . There is no choice here.

As much as Calvin and Kuyper influenced Chuck Colson and his work, William Wilberforce's impact on the ministry and its leader was still greater. As Tom Pratt, former president of Prison Fellowship advised, "To understand Chuck Colson and Prison Fellowship, you have to understand William Wilberforce."

Colson's own comments underscore the point:

> In his deep convictions, his perseverance, his industry, and his imagination, William Wilberforce provides an unparalleled example of true Christian service in a fallen world. Despite the allurements of power and position, of friends and family, and of every sort of distraction the world could offer, Wilberforce gave himself to his cause and became for us a model of selfless endurance against every sort of adversity. In later years he would be acknowledged as the greatest and most influential figure of his time, "the Washington of humanity."

William Wilberforce was born into a wealthy and locally prominent family in the Yorkshire city of Hull in 1759. He attended Cambridge where he became friends with fellow student and future British prime minister William Pitt. The two of them entered the House of Commons together in 1780, when Wilberforce was only twenty-one years old.

In 1787 he began what would be his lifelong quest to outlaw slavery in the British Empire. His detractors believed first of all that slavery was economically essential to sustain Britain's far-flung empire. There were members of Parliament who claimed to sympathize with Wilberforce's humanitarian arguments, but insisted that there was no alternative.

They further believed that Wilberforce's arguments were faith-based and therefore irrelevant in a political context (an objection Colson would often hear as well). As the second Viscount Melbourne, William Lamb, famously complained, "Things have come to a pretty pass when religion is allowed to invade public life!"

Wilberforce took a roundabout route to his faith. Early in life he had a deep interest in Christianity. He moved in with his aunt and uncle, Hannah and William Wilberforce, at age eight after his father died. That household was both pious and socially prominent, welcoming John Newton among other noteworthy preachers for sermons in their home. The story of Newton, a former slave ship captain who wrote the hymn "Amazing Grace," helped young William understand that true Christianity went beyond spiritual ideas to faith-based action.

Wilberforce's mother didn't appreciate having her son exposed to such notions. Elizabeth Wilberforce feared the "uncontrollable passions" of evangelical worship and brought him back home after two years. She believed that under his uncle's roof, little William was taking religion too much to heart: reading the Bible, avoiding the theater (notorious for the prostitutes who solicited there), and being distracted by spiritual thoughts. She made it her business to "cure" him of his overexposure to evangelical Christianity by discouraging him from pursuing it and forcing him to attend the theater as fashion required. William held on to his precocious spiritual maturity for a time, but finally abandoned it for the secular worldview his mother insisted upon.

Wilberforce regained his Christian outlook during and after a tour of the Continent in 1784–1785. Planning the trip with members of his family, he invited Isaac Milner, a former tutor of his, to keep him company. One day on the road Wilberforce happened to see a book of his cousin's, *The Rise and Progress of Religion in the Soul*, by Philip Doddridge. It was one of Milner's favorites, and the two of them discussed the book. Their exchange prompted Wilberforce to consult the Bible to see if it said what Doddridge claimed it did.

Back home in England, Wilberforce continued his season of questions and introspection. He began an intense Bible study with his uncle's old friend John Newton. On Good Friday 1786, he took communion for the first time, resolving to live his life according to the Bible.

A little more than a year later, on Sunday, October 28, 1787, he wrote in his diary, "God Almighty has set before me two great objects, the suppression of the slave trade and the reformation of manners [an eighteenth-century term for "morals"]. As biographer Kevin Belmonte wrote, "From that time forward, he would pursue these objects with a determination unprecedented in the history of his country."

Wilberforce's plans to introduce a bill outlawing the slave trade in Britain and its colonies were interrupted by a serious illness. Thinking he might die, Wilberforce convinced his friend Pitt to enter the legislation in his place. The bill languished in the House for a year until Wilberforce finally gathered the strength to speak; he gave a three-hour oration. Year after year, he pressed his case with no action being taken until 1791 when the bill came up for a vote at last and was soundly defeated.

Repeatedly Wilberforce introduced his legislation and repeatedly it was knocked down one way or another. Finally in 1796, nine years after his first attempt, the bill was approved on two of the required three readings. On the third reading it was defeated seventy-four to seventy. Wilberforce was heartbroken, not only because of his loss but because his friends seemed not to care sufficiently about it to attend the vote. "Enough were at the opera to carry it," he said dejectedly.

He wrote John Newton to say he thought perhaps he should get out of politics and pursue his Christian walk some other way. Newton insisted he was in the best place possible. He advised, "You are not only a representative for Yorkshire, you have the far greater honor of being a representative for the Lord, in a place where many know Him not, and an opportunity of showing them what are the genuine fruits of that religion which you are known to profess."

Wilberforce kept his seat in Parliament and reintroduced his abolition bill every year: every year it was deferred or defeated. Gradually, tirelessly, Wilberforce won over his opponents. Small and delicate in appearance—he was only five feet tall—Wilberforce withstood agonizing bouts of intestinal trouble. The opium doctors prescribed to alleviate his pain seriously damaged his eyesight. Yet he persevered.

Investigations into the way slaves were transported and treated revealed the horrible conditions they suffered. Momentum finally began to build in his favor. At last at 4:00 a.m. on February 24, 1807, after debating all night, the House of Commons passed a bill by 283 to 16 abolishing the slave trade in the British Empire.

Twenty years of tireless effort had finally paid off. But rather than take a well deserved rest, Wilberforce and his colleagues plunged almost immediately into the fight to abolish slavery altogether. He became a world-renowned figure. In 1814 on a visit to London, Czar Alexander of Russia requested Wilberforce to call on him.

Even after retiring from the House, suffering severe financial distress at the hands of his profligate and careless oldest son, and dealing with ever more serious illnesses, he fought on to rid the empire of slavery. In the spring of 1833 the new colonial secretary, Lord Stanley, introduced legislation to end slavery and compensate owners for their losses with government payments totaling twenty million pounds, equal to almost a billion dollars in today's buying power.

On July 26, William Wilberforce received word that a bill for abolishing slavery throughout the British colonies was assured of becoming law. He died three days later.

Wilberforce's description of those who misrepresent Christian teaching as relative rather than absolute, published posthumously in 1851, rings out strong and clear a century and a half later:

> The truth is, their opinions on the subjects of religion are not formed from the perusal of the word of God. The Bible lies on the shelf unopened; and they would be wholly ignorant of its contents, except for what they hear occasionally at church, or for the faint traces which their memories may still retain of the lessons of their earliest infancy.
>
> How different, nay, in many respects how contradictory, would be the two systems of mere mortals, of which the one should be formed from the commonly received maxims of the Christian world, and the

other from the study of the Holy Scriptures! It would be curious to remark in any one, who had hitherto satisfied himself with the former, the astonishment which would be excited on his first introduction to the latter.

Wilberforce's health, never robust, kept him bedridden for months at a time. After his eldest son lost the family fortune, Wilberforce was forced to rent out his beautiful home with its treasured library and garden and move to smaller quarters. His two daughters died young. His political enemies slandered him mercilessly. And yet he never wavered in his resolve because he felt God's calling.

In 1989 Prison Fellowship instituted the Wilberforce Award to each year honor a man or woman who is tirelessly, selflessly, and completely dedicated to advancing Christian principles in the culture in the Wilberforce tradition. The first award was given posthumously to Benigno S. Aquino, Jr., a Filipino journalist and statesman whose steadfast faith drew him to the center of a national crisis and ultimately made him a national hero.

"Ninoy" Aquino earned his country's Legion of Honor as a newspaper reporter during the Korean War while he was still a teenager. At age twenty-two, he was elected mayor of his hometown of Concepción. When he was thirty-four, he became the youngest elected senator in Philippine history. Days before a presidential election that Aquino was widely expected to win, President Ferdinand Marcos, ineligible to run for reelection, declared martial law and had him arrested.

In 1980, after seven years in prison, Aquino was freed to go to America for heart surgery under the condition that he would never return. He took his family to Boston but vowed to come back, convicted most of all by a powerful conversion experience he had in prison. During a season of dark despair behind bars, Ninoy had lost all hope and wanted to die. His mother sent him a copy of Chuck Colson's book *Born Again*. "Because of it," he later said, "I was able to survive in prison."

Colson and Aquino met in 1980. "I noticed a Filipino man staring at me," Chuck said, "then he grabbed my arm. 'You're Mr. Colson! Your book changed my life!'" Aquino told his new friend he was determined to return to the Philippines, either back into politics or back into prison. "Either way," he said, "we'll start Prison Fellowship. I promised the Lord that when I walked out of prison."

On August 21, 1983, Benigno Aquino returned to Manila. Because of his immense popularity and the death threats against him, the airport was surrounded by two thousand police and military troops, supposedly to insure his safety. Walking from the airplane to the terminal, he was shot in the head and killed. Ten days later, two million people lined the city streets to honor his funeral procession. Today, August 21 is a Philippine national holiday.

Since the posthumous award was given to Aquino, the Wilberforce Award has been bestowed every year to honor someone who exemplifies the courage, sacrifice, and unwavering resolve of the Wilberforce legacy. Recent recipients have included:

- Baroness Cox of Queensberry (1995), deputy speaker of Britian's House of Lords who championed reform in the former Soviet Union and the Sudan
- Richard John Neuhaus (1998), the esteemed Catholic theologian who lent his heart and reputation to reconciling Catholics and evangelicals
- Bishop Macram Max Gassis (2000), for his heroic defense of Christianity in the Sudan
- William E. Simon (2001, posthumous), former Secretary of the Treasury who personally donated one million dollars to Prison Fellowship
- Phillip Johnson (2004), the Berkeley law professor whose Intelligent Design theory revolutionized the creation/evolution debate

Bringing these and its other worldview programs together under one umbrella, Prison Fellowship established the Wilberforce Forum in 1991 to "encourage and equip Christians to develop a clear biblical worldview that guides all aspects of their lives and builds the Church into a persuasive influence in shaping the culture."

Prison Fellowship in America had developed over the years into a ministry engaged on three fronts: teaching, equipping, and encouraging incarcerated prisoners; working on the outside with ex-offenders, their families, and others affected by crime; and defining and promoting a Christian cultural worldview to get at the moral failure responsible for crime in the first place. At the same time, Prison Fellowship attracted attention in other countries eager to duplicate its results. The ministry shied away at first from setting up any overseas operation for fear it would stretch itself too thin. PF saw a long list of reasons not to export its programs. But clearly the Lord had other plans.

[CHAPTER 13]

Unto All the World

Prison Fellowship attracted international interest from the first. Chuck's world tour when *Born Again* was published not only sold a lot of books, it gave politicians, prison officials, and Christians in other countries a glimpse of Prison Fellowship philosophy. The idea that this ex-convict and close advisor to a disgraced U.S. president might have developed a fresh approach to dealing with prison problems made foreign officials and church leaders eager to know more.

England was the first place overseas where Prison Fellowship took root. Sylvia Mary Alison, a British evangelical Christian whose husband was a member of Parliament, at Chuck's suggestion visited an in-prison seminar on a trip to the United States. She was so moved by the experience, she proposed starting a Prison Fellowship program in Great Britain. Chuck resisted the idea because he thought he and the ministry already had more than they could do in the U.S. They had a modest budget, a handful of staff, and no clout with foreign prison systems. The last thing it seemed they should do was start branching out.

But, prompted by British interest, the board of directors began considering how they might organize and run an international ministry.

George Wilson, head of the U.S. board and executive vice president of the Billy Graham Evangelical Association, believed PF should keep tight control over any foreign operation to protect Colson's name and credibility. Chuck later gave Sylvia Mary credit for resisting that plan in favor of local control for each of the foreign boards.

In his book, *Uncommon Courage,* tracing the early history of what became Prison Fellowship International, Gordon Loux described the main issues Prison Fellowship wrestled with as it considered launching its ministry in foreign countries. First, it would be hard, maybe impossible, to collect accurate information about crime rates and prison conditions there. Authorities hesitated to admit crime was a problem or that it was growing, for fear of slowing tourism or raising questions about foreign aid. There were strong incentives to hide or embellish the facts. Furthermore, getting reliable information about prison conditions was almost impossible. How could PF direct its ministry if it couldn't clearly see the need?

Another problem was PF's overtly Christian approach. In many foreign cultures Christians are a small, oppressed minority; in some such as Saudi Arabia and China, Christian evangelism is against the law. Could Christian prison reformers work with officials under these conditions?

A third challenge was finding volunteers, the backbone of Prison Fellowship. By themselves, prison chaplains and denominational staff members could accomplish relatively little. Only a network of Christian volunteers could weave together the necessary teaching and support structure that included moral accountability, life skills, job training, help for family members, post-release mentoring—the full range of Christian nurturing. Authentic Christian evangelism requires personal involvement. Would enough dedicated Christian volunteers come forward?

Fourth was the vast difference between American culture and the home lives of foreign nationals, with its inevitable cultural tensions.

Despite their best intentions, rich, white Westerners are often resented by the poor populations they are trying to help. Whether out of envy, residual effects of colonialism, or past experience being steamrolled by arrogant foreigners calling all the shots, Third World Christians tend to resist doing things the Western way. Resolving differences in local customs, history, culture, and language would eat up a lot of time and resources without any benefit to the prisoners.

Last and looming largest was the issue of money. Historically, Western money supported Western ministries abroad, which led to Western control. For Prison Fellowship abroad to be truly locally controlled, it would have to be locally funded. This was the biggest hurdle of all. Poor countries had little if anything to spend reaching out to help the most despised members of society. Should they really be required to pay their own way? Wasn't it shortsighted not to take advantage of Western wealth at least for seed money?

The first meeting of Prison Fellowship International took place in London the week of November 23, 1978, between Colson and Loux and delegations from Britain, Jordan, and Spain. A follow-up meeting in March attracted 150 British prison wardens, chaplains, church leaders, ex-offenders, and government members, who voted unanimously to establish the Prison Christian Fellowship of Great Britain. Of the occasion Colson said, "Not once in our most daring dreams had we entertained the thought of PF expanding abroad. There was just too much to do in the U.S. first. But the Holy Spirit often moves ahead of man."

In 1979 Chuck and Gordon went on an international tour to promote the film version of *Born Again*. Just as the book tour three years earlier had sparked interest in prisons around the world, the movie promotion renewed calls for Prison Fellowship satellite operations overseas. Colson and Loux met with other Christian groups in Australia, New Zealand, and Northern Ireland who were already committed to prison ministry and wanted to see Prison Fellowship at work in their corrections systems.

The American board of directors had donated funds to help start the ministry in England, and Chuck spoke dozens of times throughout Britain to stir up early support. Gordon Loux further refined Sylvia Mary Alison's idea of locally controlled ministries into its final form. Rather than operating foreign offices from Washington, Loux devised a trade association model that gave each office individual autonomy. Prison Fellowship International, he believed, should be an assembly of separate national prison ministries whose leaders and board members were residents of that country.

As Loux later wrote in *Uncommon Courage*, "The members would 'own' it, finance it, control it, and run it. The international office would be created by the national fellowships and would exist solely to serve them." If they did that, one PF board member warned, they'd better get 51 percent of the voting power of each national board or they would lose control of the ministry. "I knew what he was getting at," Loux admitted. "Control meant unity. How would we accomplish anything internationally unless some central organization set the direction and kept everyone on track?" But, as Chuck Colson wrote in his foreword to Gordon's book, Loux "held firm" and stuck to his recommendation with "stubborn" resolve.

Loux said that "the control and unity of Prison Fellowship International had to be in the Lord's hands, not ours. If He was calling all of us to participate in this ministry, we had to come together as equals and do whatever common tasks He gave us as equals. We Americans had to have the courage to let go and trust God." And so the board, at Gordon Loux's urging, set up PFI as an association of individually run national ministries that applied Prison Fellowship's biblical teaching and reform programs to their own national prison systems, independent of any American oversight. To be chartered by PF, the national ministry had to have leaders and board members from its own country.

Local control was the first of what Loux considered two crucial decisions establishing the character of PFI. The second and much more difficult one was that to be chartered by Prison Fellowship International, a ministry had to be funded by its own country. There would be no American seed money. In fact, PFI would ask chartered ministries to contribute 5 percent (later raised to 6 percent) of their revenue to the international headquarters to cover operating costs.

This decision went against the grain of most established ministries, which depended on American or Western money and endured foreign control to get it. Yet Loux and others on the PF board believed that in the long run, the foreign offices would be stronger and more effective if local groups were responsible for them and felt a sense of ownership. They admitted they believed national financing would be, in Loux's words, "taking a longer and more difficult road."

What happened instead was that PFI, officially launched in 1979 with charter members in England, Canada, Australia, New Zealand, and the Bahamas, grew faster than they ever thought possible. Word of the ministry's work soon spread to every corner of the world. In 1981 PFI received a letter from the deputy chief justice of the Supreme Court in Papua New Guinea. An Australian friend had given him copies of *Born Again* and *Life Sentence,* and after reading them the justice wanted to know how to start a Prison Fellowship ministry in his country.

"We weren't sure where Papua New Guinea was," Loux said. "We certainly didn't know anything about its culture, its crime problem, or the Christian resources available there." Six years later, Prison Fellowship New Guinea was "one of the finest prison ministries in the world," active in prisons throughout the country without any Western financial support.

If any country could claim exemption from the ban on Western funding, India seemed a likely candidate. The second most populous country in the world, overwhelmingly Hindu and poor, had more than a million people in prison. It looked like an impossible task to raise the money for Prison Fellowship India from local sources. "My heart broke as I refused" to fund the ministry there, Loux recalled, "but I reminded [them] of the parable of the sower. A seed planted in shallow ground will grow too quickly and will wither in the heat of the summer sun. To endure, the ministry of India would have to put down deep roots in its own country."

Within only a few years, Prison Fellowship India was a resounding success, with Christian volunteers visiting inmates in eight hundred prisons across the country. Though prison officials were mostly Hindu, they enthusiastically supported the program because they saw first-hand how dramatically the Christian gospel changed inmates' lives. Ironically, though public Christian discipleship and outreach are restricted in India, Christians shared their witness boldly in prisons nationwide, thanks entirely to Indian Christians and Indian financial support.

Prison Fellowship International served its local chartered members first of all with practical assistance: training conferences, seminars, teaching resources, fund-raising help, and volunteer recruitment. PFI also helped develop an active Christian ministry in each country. As Gordon Loux explained,

> Our ministry is based on the conviction that the only real hope for the problems of our criminal justice system, the only real hope for the reformation of criminal offenders, is the redemptive and reconciling power of Jesus Christ mediated through the Christian community. The statement of faith is nonnegotiable. It must be formally accepted by every national ministry belonging to Prison Fellowship International. It defines who we are, why we exist, where our power comes from, and where our hope lies.

Another objective of PFI was to encourage criminal justice reform according to biblical standards, using some of the same arguments that were beginning to find a sympathetic audience in America—community service, restitution, and reconciliation instead of prison terms for nonviolent criminals.

Though the international crime rate was rising overall, incarceration rates were lower in countries with high levels of community involvement in prison operations. Countries with some of the lowest crime rates, such as Japan, also had low incarceration rates, while the rate was high in countries where proportionally more citizens were in prison, such as the United States. Around the world, most crimes were committed by ex-offenders. Prison conditions were even more of a school for criminals overseas than in the U.S.

Hoping to improve its visibility and credibility with foreign governments and access to their prisons, Prison Fellowship International applied for membership in the United Nations Economic and Social Council in February 1983. This council, a worldwide forum for nongovernmental organizations, consists only of groups whose operations, objectives, and results meet the strict and sometimes capricious standards of member nations.

To PFI vice president of administration Kathryn Grant, who shepherded the application through the arduous process, the prospects for approval looked dim. Ninety NGOs were applying for membership. The French were unforgiving of the least little error or inconsistency in form and style of the complex application paperwork. Pakistan and the USSR challenged every applicant with a strong religious affiliation. The committee rejected one organization in business twenty-five years for "lack of experience."

To Kathryn's relief and delight, the French delegate fully endorsed the PF application, saying, "I have looked over this organization's application. It is well done. Furthermore, I have read Charles Colson's books, and I approve of his work. This organization has great credit. I strongly recommend they receive full membership."

Her joy was short-lived. The USSR and Pakistan opposed the application. After some discussion the full committee offered PFI nonvoting membership. To Kathryn a nonvoting membership, though prestigious, was very little use practically. It would be a great victory for the ministry, a coming of age in international socio-political affairs, but by accepting a nonvoting membership, now she ran the risk of never winning a full voting membership.

She turned the UN down.

The next day the Prison Fellowship International application came up for final disposition. The offer of nonvoting membership had been declined. After an interminable moment of silence, the representative from Pakistan withdrew his objection and agreed to full membership. Before the Soviet member could speak, the committee chairman gaveled approval. PF was in.

Only a few months earlier, Ron Nikkel had left an executive position with Youth for Christ in Canada to join PFI as vice president for field operations. "I wasn't interested at first" in leaving YFC, Nikkel said. But after a meeting with the Prison Fellowship leadership, he agreed to take the position if the organization was truly international "and not just a U.S.-based organization with international purposes."

Nikkel's first major project was setting up the inaugural Prison Fellowship International worldwide conference in Belfast, Northern Ireland, in 1983. Delegates from thirty-four nations attended. "PFI was totally unknown then," Nikkel said, "but Chuck was the drawing card." Everybody, it seemed, wanted to see and hear the famous author and Watergate "celebrity."

Belfast was a dangerous place where longstanding political and religious tensions had erupted in violence. Northern Ireland, part of the United Kingdom, had been separated from the Catholic Republic of Ireland in 1920 and joined to Protestant Great Britain. Catholics in the officially Protestant north resolved to reunite with the Republic, touching off a bloody civil upheaval.

The location made for symbolic comparison: an organization dedicated to international spiritual renewal and forgiveness holding its first-ever conference in one of the most violent and bloody cities in the Western world. Delegates met in the elegant Malone House, recently rebuilt after damage from a Catholic terrorist bombing.

The speakers gave simple, heartfelt testimonials that drove home the special power of God behind bars even in so dangerous and brutal a place. One man was introduced as Liam O'Donnell (a pseudonym to protect him from reprisals), a prisoner paroled for the evening. He had started his sentence in the notorious Maze Prison, one of the dirtiest and most violent prisons in the kingdom, a relic out of Dickens. He had joined in a "blanket protest," during which prisoners refused to wear any clothes. Later he was part of the infamous "dirty protest," when prisoners refused to wash or leave their cells to answer the calls of nature. Within a few days the stench made even the guards vomit. No outsiders would come near the place.

After that Liam committed himself to a hunger strike. Ten Maze prisoners starved themselves to death, driven by a lifetime of hatred for the British and their official Protestantism. Liam was the eleventh hunger strike volunteer. After seven weeks without food, he was blind and too weak to sit up in bed. With certain death only hours away, his mother ordered him fed intravenously on day fifty-five.

In time, his sight returned and he was able to walk, though with a pronounced limp due to permanent muscle damage. The experience forced him to consider what was truly important in the world. "I realized you cannot serve two masters," he told the hushed audience. He explained he'd decided to serve Christ, which meant he could no longer serve the Republican movement. Like giving up a gang membership, renouncing the Irish Republican fight could have been a self-imposed death sentence; other pro-Republic fighters in the prison might easily have killed him. What saved him was the credibility he earned with his former companions through the hunger strike.

His Republican partisans were astonished soon afterward to see him violate an absolutely inviolable taboo—sitting with Protestants at a meal. What surprised them even more was when he told them he was swearing off retribution. Once Liam O'Donnell dedicated his life to Christ alone, there was no pride, no earthly loyalty to keep him from extending the hand of friendship to his lifelong enemies, even if his cellmates killed him for it. His gesture started breaking down barriers between the two sides that seemed unassailable. By choosing Christ, he pointed the way to reconciliation for every prisoner behind the dark walls of Maze.

A second speaker at the conference was Pearl McKeown. Quietly she told the story of her teenage daughter Karen, who was shot on the street at random by the Irish Republican Army. Before she died ten days later, she left her Bible to her murderer so he would know she had forgiven him. Pearl's faith had plumbed new depths and reached new heights since her daughter's bequest. Her husband, Karen's father, became a Christian because of Karen's testimony.

The Belfast meeting established a PFI tradition of assembling every few years to encourage and exhort each other, pray together, and share ideas and techniques. At the second international convocation in Nairobi in 1986, keynote speaker Cardinal Jaime Sin, Archbishop of Manila, encouraged his audience:

> If there is any illusion that is shattered in prison, it is man's self-suf-
> ficiency. Incarceration is a radical experience of helplessness. . . . This
> can, of course, be a devastating realization. But it can also be a singu-
> lar opportunity for the breakthrough of saving truth. It is that crucial
> point where man's hand clasps the hand of God and weakness turns
> into strength.

At the 1995 meeting, in Washington, D.C., sixty-nine chartered ministries (those officially sanctioned by and supporters of PFI) participated with representatives from 124 countries in all. One Muslim prison official there from Nigeria had originally resisted PFI. Later he allowed volunteers into the prisons and sat in on part of their presentation. At the end he called the PFI workers into his office, fell on his knees, and received Christ.

The city of Sofia hosted the 1999 meeting, attended by chartered ministries from 88 nations (by the time of the 2004 conference in Toronto there would be 105 chartered members). The most captivating speaker in the Bulgarian capital was not a fiery clergyman or powerful politician, but a demure soft-spoken woman named Kim Puc. Her name was unfamiliar, but her picture was seared into the collective memory of the Vietnam era. She was the burned child in the iconic photograph of the war, running naked and screaming from a napalm attack on her village.

Repairing her burns took seventeen surgeries. After that she worked for the Vietnamese propaganda machine, stirring up hatred of America and the West. Then her life was transformed by the message of Christ. Fearing for her safety and determined to practice Christianity in the open, she found asylum in Canada. "It was the fire of bombs which burned my body," she said. "It was the skill of doctors which mended my skin. But it took the power of God's love to heal my heart."

PFI raised up inspiring native Christian leaders like Jorge Martinez, president of Prison Fellowship El Salvador. A successful lawyer in the capital city of San Salvador, he was an outwardly happy man who lived an empty, meaningless life inside. One day he prayed, "God, I don't believe in you, but I would like to. If you exist, give me faith." God soon answered his prayer, filling him with a sense of peace and a desire to share Jesus with others.

Only a month later, Martinez was kidnapped at his office by thugs working for one of his clients' competitors. For eight days they held him captive, repeatedly tying a plastic bag around his head until he was near the point of death, removing the bag just in time to keep him from suffocating. Shortly after they released him, the captors came back to his office. Fearful at first, Martinez grew amazed as he listened to their story. They had been impressed by his calm endurance and returned to ask his forgiveness. Jorge explained that his faith carried him through the painful and life-threatening ordeal. He would forgive them, he said, but real forgiveness came only from God. His witness led several of his former kidnappers to Christ.

Javier Bustamante, regional director for PFI in South America and former head of the largest prison in Peru, demonstrated the power of prayer by calling on Christ in a time of need. He sat down with a group in Ecuador that wanted to start a Prison Fellowship ministry. Beginning the meeting with great anticipation, he quickly sensed that the men were "divided and immature in their faith." Dejected, he went back to his hotel and spent most of the night in prayer.

The next morning while Javier was eating breakfast, a bellboy noticed the Bible beside him and interrupted him. "I'm a Christian too," he said smiling, then asked what Bustamante was doing in town.

"I'm here to consider starting a prison ministry," he answered.

The astounded bellboy said, "I don't believe it! Just last night our fellowship prayed that God would send us someone to help us begin a work in the prison!" Though it wasn't the group he'd come to see, Bustamante unexpectedly found an eager new band of co-laborers for his work.

In the mid-1980s, Chuck Colson and Ron Nikkel were in Trivandrum, in southern India, where Chuck spoke to inmates in the prison through a translator. At first the audience stared suspiciously, but when he started talking about a man with brown skin like theirs who was thrown into prison, Colson said, "The inmates leaned forward, straining to catch every word. Their eyes soon grew big, their expressions full of wonder. I told them that Christ had gone to the cross and died for their sins, and that they could be forgiven and have a new life. . . . I have never seen any crowd anywhere suddenly become so responsive to my message."

After a prayer, Chuck was preparing to walk out of the room when, on impulse, he stepped off the speaking platform and shook hands with the man closest to him. Since prisoners are at the bottom of India's ancient social caste system, touching them is considered unclean.

Suddenly the crowd rose up like a flock of birds and approached him, forming a circle around him and politely taking turns to step forward and shake his hand or touch him.

Years later, in 2001, Colson spoke to a meeting of ten thousand Third World evangelists in Amsterdam. The next day a man introduced himself to Chuck as one of the prisoners he had touched in Trivandrum. Released after fourteen years, he was an outcast and so were his children. Quietly resisting the social taboos against prisoners in responsible positions, he and his wife had begun running the PFI Precious Children's Home in Bangalore, even though some officials there refused to speak to him. It was a refuge for mistreated, outcast, or abandoned children of prisoners who otherwise faced malnutrition, homelessness, and sexual exploitation.

PFI ministries set up similar homes for prisoners' children in other countries. Peace Loving Children's Home, established by PFI Nepal, became so popular that a second home was opened there. The Nepalese ministry also built a rehabilitation center for ex-prisoners. True to the original vision of local control, all these Christian projects were fully funded by one of the poorest countries in the world—and a predominantly Hindu one at that.

After Gordon Loux resigned from PFI in 1988, Ron Nikkel succeeded him as president. As the international ministry's longest serving leader, Nikkel has traveled literally millions of miles to interconnect PFI ministries around the world. "God surprises me every day," he said, "including everything from local gourmet delicacies to the power of one person's faith."

On one visit he found himself as the guest of honor where he was served the greatest delicacy in the house—blood-gorged leeches. He passed them to another man at the table, insisting he was the guest of honor. Another time, in India, he met with a man from Sri Lanka who had written earlier, asking if Nikkel would meet with him. Ron later learned that the man had sold his kitchen stove to pay for his trip. Soon the man spearheaded the founding of Prison Fellowship Sri Lanka.

In an interview in 2003, Ron shared the best advice anyone ever gave him. It was from Mike Timmis, chairman of the board of PFI, who admonished him to keep Jesus at the center of everything. "If you are not growing closer to Jesus in this ministry," Timmis advised, "get out."

Headquartered near Washington, D.C., PFI today has regional offices in Zimbabwe, Singapore, Switzerland, Peru, and New Zealand. Along with prison ministry in thousands of institutions, PFI also sponsors the Global Assistance Program. Since 1995, this program has sent more than six hundred volunteer medical professionals to treat ninety-five thousand members of the international prison community, standing in the gap by serving Christ among the poorest of the poor.

Another worldwide outreach is the GEO trust, a micro-lending program providing small start-up loans to qualified ex-prisoners to help them start small businesses in order to "restore ex-prisoners to responsible and productive relationships with their families, communities, and with their Creator." There's also Sycamore Tree, a ministry that brings victims into prisons to talk to offenders and discuss the consequences of crime. In eight to twelve week sessions, prisoners learn firsthand how crime affects an individual's life. Perhaps for the first time ever, they see the cost of their actions in human terms. Though criminals and victims who participate are never "related" by the same incident, meeting through Sycamore Tree gives them a personal perspective that promotes forgiveness on one side and rehabilitation on the other.

Prison Fellowship International has flourished in large countries and small, in Christian cultures, as well as corners of the world, where Christians are an unwelcome minority. More than one hundred thousand volunteers a year serve prisoners in the name of Jesus through PFI, uniting a dazzling variety of cultures and governments behind a message of justice, hope, and compassion.

[CHAPTER 14]

Coming of Age

A s the ministry of Prison Fellowship extended its reach across the country and around the world, the Washington-based headquarters staff scrambled to keep one step ahead of the expansion. More and bigger programs required more people, more room, more money, and more sophisticated publicity and public relations. Behind the scenes, the PF leadership worked hard to ensure that the programs didn't outrun their financial and administrative support structure, and that the ministry took advantage of every opportunity to enhance its public profile.

A year after launching the ministry from three basement rooms in Arlington, Virginia, Chuck and the staff had moved to larger space in McLean, added a second office suite there a year later, and then started looking for a building they could buy. An empty church was for sale, but neighbors objected to having a prison ministry nearby. They heard rumors that the building would be a halfway house, or that criminals would be running loose in the streets. Rather than fight, Prison Fellowship gave up the opportunity and kept looking.

PF finally bought a rambling old house in Great Falls that was converted into office space. Modest though it was, it had the advantage of being across the street from Thelma's Ice Cream Parlor, a favorite local hangout. Buying a building seemed like a stretch at the time, but soon the headquarters was bursting at the seams as the ministry added workers to keep up with new demands. The paid staff remained as small as possible, with volunteers continuing to shoulder most of the load. For the first eight years, Chuck Colson not only drew no salary, but he continued donating book and film royalties to offset expenses.

After the Great Falls headquarters was filled to overflowing, PF housed workers in rented space nearby. Prison Fellowship International also moved out to separate quarters to help relieve the overcrowding.

Scouring northern Virginia for a new headquarters, building committee chairman David Cauwels, a successful New Mexico businessman and longtime friend of the ministry, despaired at ever finding enough land for a headquarters so close to Washington. Because most of their work involved government agencies, PF wanted to stay within reasonable driving distance of the District of Columbia. But land prices anywhere near the capital were some of the highest in the country. The question was how they would ever find room enough, close enough, at a price they could afford.

As Cauwels and his committee kept looking and praying, a solution emerged from an unexpected quarter. Developers had bought the last few remaining acres of an old estate in Reston, Virginia, with plans to build a ten-story luxury hotel. The project went bust and an offshore bank put the land up for sale. (One of the partners later went to prison and PF volunteers visited him there.) The property was a tranquil island of a little more than five acres surrounding a historic home built in 1899 by Dr. A. Smith Bowman. The gas stations and shopping centers lining the overgrown perimeter were once part of Dr. Bowman's seventy-two-thousand-acre estate called Sunset Hills.

The house had been vacant seven years, weathered but sound. And there was plenty of room behind it to build a headquarters with all the offices, meeting space, storage, mailroom, audio-visual, development, hospitality, and other operations the ministry needed under one roof. Prison Fellowship bought the property in 1983, then started restoring the old home and raising money for a new office complex.

Groundbreaking for the new headquarters was January 30, 1985, the same day the beautifully refurbished Bowman place was dedicated as DeMoss House in honor of insurance executive Arthur S. DeMoss, a generous supporter of the ministry who had advised, "Attempt something so impossible that unless God is in it, it is doomed to failure." For almost twenty years—until the ministry's next move in 2004—DeMoss House would welcome distinguished overnight visitors to Prison Fellowship.

Only a short time after PF purchased the Reston acreage, government authorities announced plans for a toll road from Washington to the new Dulles Airport that would pass less than a mile from it. Land values along the right-of-way skyrocketed overnight. A few weeks later and the Bowman estate or any other property in the region would have been completely out of reach.

In June 1987, Chuck Colson, Dave Cauwels, and the entire Prison Fellowship family gratefully dedicated the new headquarters complex just over the hill from DeMoss House. There were two low-rise brick office buildings connected by an enclosed walk, an expansive patio, and beautifully landscaped grounds. For the first time in years, all the components of the ministry were under one roof with room to spare.

But it was also a rocky time, when the ministry faced a crisis in leadership, and when Colson faced the consequences of a life-threatening illness.

Gordon Loux was an early member of the PF leadership inner circle with the theological perspective as well as the communications skills to move the ministry forward. When Chuck decided to step down as president in 1984, Gordon lobbied hard for, and won, the job as his successor. Problems soon bubbled to the surface. What had been a cordial but hectic working environment grew tense. Chuck blamed himself for putting Loux in a job that didn't match his skills and abilities.

At this critical juncture, Chuck was diagnosed with a stomach tumor. The doctors thought he might have cancer and advised surgery as soon as possible. They removed the tumor in January 1987; because a preliminary operating room biopsy indicated cancer, the surgeon also removed part of Colson's stomach. Chuck spent an extended time in the hospital with an infection and post-operative complications. It would eventually take two years and another operation for him to completely heal.

Still weak, Colson returned to work after his first surgery to find Prison Fellowship in what he described as "chaos." "Good people were quitting," he saw with alarm, "and everybody was grumbling and unhappy." Colson also learned that while he was in the hospital, Loux had fired someone whom they had discussed at length and whom Colson told him "not to fire under any circumstances." Loux's position was that it was inevitable the employee would be let go, so it made sense to do so before PF moved into its new Reston offices instead of immediately afterward; he didn't want to disturb Chuck in the hospital in order to discuss it further.

Whether misunderstanding or misstep, the incident lay heavy on Chuck's heart. He was still in pain and worried about the prospect of recurring cancer, lying awake at night wondering whether he would die before Prison Fellowship collapsed or vice versa. "It was a low point in the ministry," he said.

Colson met with Loux in Washington. "I told Gordon we had to make a change," he solemnly recalled, after which Loux graciously resigned. Back home, Colson felt "wretched" over what had happened. He called Gordon to talk some more and within minutes they were both crying. "I said, 'I tried so hard.' It broke my heart to see that happen because I still loved Gordon and I know he loved the ministry."

Colson's long-time friend Al Quie, the former congressman and governor of Minnesota, took over as acting president. "He did a magnificent job calming the place down, getting it back on track spiritually, and really giving strong leadership," Colson said of Quie. The ex-governor flew in from Minnesota three days a week, living in the DeMoss House. Confident that Al could run things smoothly, Chuck began to withdraw more from daily operations to concentrate on writing, outreach, and strategic development. In 1987, at the board's urging, Chuck and Patty Colson moved from Virginia to Florida.

Colson and the board also began the serious work of finding a permanent president. The man Chuck thought was best for the job, board member Tom Pratt, wasn't interested. In fact he had planned to step off the board altogether until his friend and fellow board member Dois Rosser encouraged him to stay on. Pratt thought it over and changed his mind. "The fellowship was so sweet I decided I shouldn't step down," he said later.

Chuck described Tom Pratt as "my likeliest candidate right from the beginning," but he couldn't blame him for turning down the offer. Pratt was a corporate officer at Herman Miller, designers and manufacturers of high-end office furniture. He was on the Herman Miller gift committee and had joined the Prison Fellowship board to monitor how his company's substantial donations were spent.

After a yearlong recruiting search, Chuck and Patty invited Tom and his wife, Gloria, to visit them in Florida and talk about Tom's prospects with PF one more time. The Pratts had a very substantial income, a beautiful house, and lived near their children and grandchildren. There was no reason to leave it all behind to run a prison ministry. During Saturday afternoon tea at the Ritz Carlton, they decided not to make the move. But when they finished packing in their hotel the next morning, Tom turned suddenly to his wife and asked, "Are you in the same place we were yesterday?" Gloria answered, "I don't know. Where are you?"

"Well, we could go on to be the president of Herman Miller and be miserable."

In that moment, he had a sudden, unsettling sense of what it would be like to be outside the will of God.

"I don't know if we're called to this," Tom continued, "but I feel like we shouldn't say no and let the Lord show us what he wants us to do from here."

To Colson's surprise and delight, Tom accepted the job. Tom's resolve was tested a few months later when Herman Miller invited him back to replace the CEO. He broke the news to Colson during the 1989 Florida governor's prayer breakfast. Hearing the offer, Chuck expected to be looking for a new president again soon. But a week later Tom told him he believed he had made the right decision and would continue with the ministry. "I will be forever grateful as long as I live to Tom Pratt and Gloria," Chuck said. "They made a huge sacrifice, came in and really saved the ministry. Tom was a disciplined, tough-minded executive, but also a gentle and loving guy. He was just what Prison Fellowship needed."

Tom set his standards for the ministry high, and he set them early. He learned that two headquarters staff members, both star employees and ex-offenders, were involved in affairs and "tawdry behavior." After determining that they had lost their moral authority to lead, he quickly fired them. Taking a step further, he announced to the rest of the staff why these two were dismissed, and that he would hold all of them to the highest standards of moral behavior. "I was at the meeting," Colson said. "It was tense to say the least. But it turned things around in Prison Fellowship." Chuck remembered several cases of "moral failure and potential embarrassment" up to that time, "but I honestly can think of only one other we've had from that day to this, which Tom handled as well. He straightened out the ship."

The fired employees filed lawsuits against Pratt and Colson personally, setting off two years of legal wrangling. A resounding defeat could have cost Colson everything he owned and his ministry besides. In the end, both he and Pratt were completely cleared. (One of the plaintiffs later sought reconciliation and consideration for another job. It didn't work out.)

One of the ministry's greatest honors and its most prominent moment in the world spotlight came in 1993 when Charles Colson received the Templeton Prize for Progress in Religion. The award, given annually to the nominee, Christian or non-Christian, whom the selection committee believes did the most to advance the world's understanding of religion, is sponsored by British financier Sir John Templeton. The prize has been awarded to Pope John Paul II, Mother Teresa, Alexander Solzhenitsyn, Billy Graham, and other world-renowned figures.

The first Chuck knew of his achievement was a call from his friend George Gallup who told him, "I voted for you for the Templeton Prize." Later when a man Colson had never heard of, Wilbert Faulkner, called representing the Templeton Foundation and asked for a meeting, Colson assumed he wanted to know his opinion of a nominee. But during their lunch at a Naples, Florida, restaurant near Chuck's home, Faulkner revealed that Chuck had been chosen to receive the prize.

The award was a million dollars, tax free. Faulkner's first question after delivering the news was, "Who do you want the check made out to?" With perhaps only a beat of hesitation Colson replied, "Prison Fellowship," consistent with his longtime practice of donating royalties from his book sales to the ministry. "After all," he said, "I'm not writing about myself. I'm writing about the Lord."

The money was a providential windfall for the ministry, which had been struggling financially. Jack Eckerd had offered a $2 million challenge grant to put the ministry back on solid footing. If the rest of the leadership team could come up with $2 million, Eckerd would match it for a total of $4 million. The board had stalled at about a million dollars. Colson's Templeton Prize money was key to reaching the goal and triggering Eckerd's generous contribution.

Chuck kept his award quiet for two months until it was officially announced at the United Nations in New York. Prison Fellowship became front-page and prime-time news around the country—a tremendous boost for the ministry. Colson received the award from Prince Philip, husband of Queen Elizabeth II of Great Britain, in a private ceremony at Buckingham Palace on May 12, 1993.

Chuck had been admonished repeatedly by Sir John Templeton not to go over his allotted two minutes at the palace, so he spoke a minute about his own faith journey and another minute about prison ministry. Then the prince started asking questions, including what Britain could do to reduce juvenile crime. "That's easy," Colson answered. "Send more of them to Sunday School." The prince and everyone else in the room laughed, but Colson said, "No, I'm serious," and summarized a study showing that juvenile crime in England was lowest when Sunday School attendance was highest. "You know," the prince replied thoughtfully, "that's a very good idea."

Altogether, Colson and Prince Philip talked back and forth for more than half an hour in front of the assembled group, far beyond Chuck's allotted two minutes. Colson observed, "All the time Sir John looked like he was about to have kittens because he thought we were dragging it on . . . but Prince Philip seemed really engaged. So it was a wonderful occasion." It was Chuck who finally said, "Your royal highness, you've been very kind to us and gracious. We don't want to hold you here," bringing the extraordinary exchange to an end.

The public ceremony awarding the prize was on September 2, before the World Parliament of Religions at McCormick Chapel in Chicago. The announcement that Colson, a renowned conservative apologist, would speak before this pluralistic, multicultural, theologically liberal religious group brought, in Colson's words, "an absolute uproar from the evangelical community. To them, this body was the big Satan, and no self-respecting Christian could ever speak to them. It was, by the way, the one-hundredth anniversary of their first meeting, when the speaker was Dwight L. Moody, a point no one among my detractors made."

Chuck continued, "I realized that the crowd would not be particularly friendly or receptive." Since the Templeton speech was generally printed and broadcast around the world he wanted to be at his best and longed for a friendly audience. "My assistant, Jim Jewell, came up with the bright idea of packing the hall," Chuck said, "but the Templeton people wouldn't give us any tickets. So Jim went out and printed a thousand of them, and we distributed them to our friends all over the Chicago and Indiana area. The result was that the hall was absolutely packed, and the crowd was fifty-fifty mainline World Parliament of Religions and Colson friends."

It was the opportunity of a lifetime for him and for his ministry. Into the moment, Colson poured almost twenty years of Christian study and service, ably assisted by Mike Gerston, who later became a speech writer for President George W. Bush. The result was a speech that still stands as perhaps the most articulate and complete apologetic for Prison Fellowship ever given.

To an international audience representing eighteen faiths, Colson made his position clear from the first words: "I speak as one transformed by Jesus Christ, the living God," he began. "He is the Way, the Truth and the Life. . . . His presence is the sole explanation for whatever is praiseworthy in my work."

He went on to discuss four great myths of our time, the four horsemen of the present apocalypse: the goodness of man, the promise of coming utopia, the relativity of moral values, and radical individualism. "These myths," he said, "constitute a threat for all of us, regardless of our culture or the faith communities we represent. . . . Modernity was once judged by the heights of its aspirations. Today it must be judged by the depth of its decadence. That decadence has marked the West most deeply; this makes it imperative that we understand the struggle for the soul of Western civilization."

The consequence of this decadence, he continued, had been an explosion in crime. "For criminals are not made by sociological or environmental or economic forces. They are created by their own moral choices. Institutions of cold steel and bars are unable to reach the human heart, and so they can neither deter nor rehabilitate. . . . Crime is a mirror of a community's moral state. A society cannot long survive if the demands of human dignity are not written on our hearts. No number of police can enforce order; no threat of punishment can create it. Crime and violence frustrate every political answer, because there can be no solution apart from character and creed.

"But relativism and individualism have undermined the traditional beliefs that once informed our character and defined our creed. There are no standards to guide us. Dostoyevsky's diagnosis was correct: 'Without God, everything is permissible; crime is inevitable.'"

At the very moment the Soviet Union had crumbled and the world looked more than ever to Western culture for a pathway to freedom, "the culture that fashioned this freedom is being overrun by the four horsemen. . . . Make no mistake: This humanizing, civilizing influence is the Judeo-Christian heritage [which] has laid the foundations of freedom in the West. It has established a standard of justice over both men and nations. It has proclaimed a higher law that exposes the pretensions of tyrants.

"Christian conviction inspires public virtue, the moral impulse to do good. It has sent legions into battle against disease, oppression, and bigotry. It ended the slave trade, built hospitals and orphanages, tamed the brutality of mental wards and prisons. In every age it has given divine mercy a human face in the lives of those who follow Christ.

"This is the lesson of centuries: that ordered liberty is one of faith's triumphs. And yet, western cultural and political elites seem blinded by modernity's myths to the historic civilizing role of Christian faith. And so, in the guise of pluralism and tolerance, they have set about to exile religion from our common life. They use the power of the media and the law like steel wool to scrub public debates and public places bare of religious ideas and symbols. But what is left is sterile and featureless and cold.

"These elites seek freedom without self-restraint, liberty without standards. But they find instead the revenge of offended absolutes.

"Courts strike down even perfunctory prayers, and we are surprised that schools, bristling with barbed wire, look more like prisons than prisons do.

"Universities reject the very idea of truth, and we are shocked when the best and the brightest of their graduates loot and betray.

"Celebrities mock the traditional family, even revile it as a form of slavery, and we are appalled at the human tragedy of broken homes and millions of unwed mothers.

"The media celebrate sex without responsibility, and we are horrified by sexual plagues.

"Our lawmakers justify the taking of innocent life in sterile clinics, and we are terrorized by the disregard for life in blood-soaked streets.

"Admittedly the signs are not auspicious . . . and it is easy to become discouraged. But a Christian has neither the reason nor the right, for history's cadence is called with a confident voice. The God of Abraham, Isaac, and Jacob reigns. His play and purpose rob the future of its fears.

"By the Cross He offers hope, by the Resurrection He assures His triumph. This cannot be resisted or delayed. Mankind's only choice is to recognize Him now or in the moment of ultimate judgment. Our only decision is to welcome His rule or to fear it.

"But this gives every one of us hope. For this is a vision beyond a vain utopia or a timid new world order. It is the vision of an Enduring Revolution. One that breaks down more than the chains of tyranny; it breaks the chains of sin and death. And it proclaims a liberation that the cruelest prison cannot contain."

Of the historic evening Colson said, "I was exhausted because I had given the speech a dry run at four o'clock and McCormick Chapel was swelteringly hot. But when the event came off that evening it was absolutely remarkable. The Holy Spirit took over [and] the effect on the audience was absolutely extraordinary. I've never seen anything like it. There was a standing ovation, precipitated I'm sure by the Colson friends, but the whole World Parliament joined, and it was widely reported afterwards that I had boldly proclaimed the gospel to a hostile group."

This season atop the high mountain, basking in the glow of recognition and public favor, was short lived. Over the next two years, Prison Fellowship experienced a pair of crises that brought the ministry to a low point and raised concerns about its very ability to survive.

[CHAPTER 15]

The Refiner's Fire

The first crisis had a very long fuse. Back in 1985, Chuck had organized a meeting of religious leaders, educators, and theologians to
hear presentations from Reverend Richard John Neuhaus, of the
Institute on Religion and Public Life, and Carl F. H. Henry, editor and
founder of *Christianity Today* magazine. The question before them was
what they should do to respond to an increasingly secular culture
where religion was becoming irrelevant.

Though it didn't produce any plan of action at the time, this informal conclave generated ideas that simmered until 1992 when Colson,
along with Reverend Neuhaus, spearheaded a formal meeting of evangelical Protestants and Catholics. These two groups, Colson believed,
were the Christian bodies most committed to evangelism, and, at their
core, the most faithful to the fundamentals of Christian doctrine.
Obviously there were bedrock differences in theology, but Chuck
wanted to concentrate on the beliefs that united them rather than
those that divided. Together, he and others believed, they could over-
come the differences that were hampering the progress of the gospel.

On March 29, 1994, after more than a year of meetings and word-smithing, the group released a joint statement titled "Evangelicals and Catholics Together: The Christian Mission in the Third Millennium." In the press release accompanying the announcement, Chuck commented on the two Christian traditions:

> We have differences, but on the ancient creeds and the core beliefs of Christianity we stand together. Christianity is besieged on all sides— by a militant nation of Islam, by pantheists who have invaded many areas of life through the New Age Movement, and by the aggressive secularism of Western life.

The joint statement acknowledged the deep differences between Catholics and Protestants going back to the Reformation and specifically listed a number of key areas. Among them: whether religious authority is in the Bible alone or as interpreted by the church; whether beliefs are rightly shaped by individual Christians or the teaching authority of the faith community; whether Christian ministry is ordered in apostolic succession or in the priesthood of all believers; whether sacraments are symbols of grace or means of grace; whether Mary is to be remembered or revered.

While admitting these divisions, the overall tenor of the statement was one of unity and cooperation, as other excerpts show. Considering the points of conflict:

> We do not presume to suggest that we can resolve the deep and long standing differences between Evangelicals and Catholics. Indeed these differences may never be resolved short of the Kingdom Come. Nonetheless, we are not permitted simply to resign ourselves to differences that divide us from one another. Not all differences are authentic disagreements, nor need all disagreements divide.

And elsewhere in the statement:

All who accept Christ as Lord and Savior are brothers and sisters in Christ. Evangelicals and Catholics are brothers and sisters in Christ. We have not chosen one another, just as we have not chosen Christ. He has chosen us, and he has chosen us to be his together. However imperfect our communion with one another, however deep our disagreements with one another, we recognize that there is but one church of Christ. There is one church because there is one Christ and the church is his body. However difficult the way, we recognize that we are called by God to a fuller realization of our unity in the body of Christ.

Colson and Neuhaus made their announcement on Maundy Thursday, the Thursday before Easter. Because it was otherwise a light news day and this was a religious story, it made headlines around the country. Colson was amazed to pick up the newspaper the next morning in Albany, New York, and see himself on the front page. As the *New York Times* reported, this notion of conspiring with Catholics "shook the evangelical world." Within a day Neuhaus observed, "Friendships and institutions were blown apart" by the news.

Evangelical Protestants blasted Colson and Prison Fellowship for consorting with Catholics, whom many of them believed were not Christian and belonged to an apostate sect. PF had some notable allies, including J. I. Packer and Bill Bright, but the clamor against them continued to grow. D. James Kennedy told Colson privately that what he'd done would destroy him. R. C. Sproul called him a heretic. "It was a tremendous, bitter reaction," Colson remembered, "a very touchy time."

Partly at the request of Joe Stohl of Moody Bible Institute, who was a friend of Colson and the ministry, D. James Kennedy and R. C. Sproul convened a meeting of evangelical leaders at Kennedy's church in Florida to discuss the issue. Colson was "summoned," he said, to what was "the closest thing I could imagine to an inquisition."

Kennedy sat at the head of a conference table with Colson and his supporters on one side and Sproul and his supporters on the other. To Chuck, his critics seemed like "hyper-reformed Calvinists" with no room for accommodation or compromise.

"We sweated it out for three or four hours," Colson said. "All the time I was thinking, 'My ministry is going down the tubes and I hate to take Prison Fellowship with me.' We got to the end of the meeting and Jim Packer came up with a wonderfully Irenic statement that the signatories could issue that we hoped would clarify and bring some peace to the issue."

But peace was elusive. Colson and his ministry continued to take a pounding. Contributions began to drop off; the ministry would eventually attribute a million-and-a-half-dollar drop in income to the controversy. "I thought ECT had blown it, ruined the ministry," Chuck said.

Out of this crisis, came what for Colson was one of the most heartwarming moments of his own spiritual journey. He called the entire home office staff into the multipurpose room at the Reston headquarters, a large, low-ceilinged space used for meetings, parties, worship services, and other gatherings. They were as worried as he was about the long-term effect of the bad publicity on Prison Fellowship.

"When I addressed the staff," Chuck said, "I told them exactly why I had done what I had done. I told them my passion and my convictions. I told them I believed I was doing exactly the right thing and it was what God wanted me to do, but I hoped I wasn't putting the whole ministry in jeopardy. I asked them just for their understanding, their prayers, and their support, that we might stand together through this crisis.

"I will never forget that moment when I just said to them, 'I hope I have your confidence and support.' The fellow sitting down front, Whitney Kunniholm, bolted out of his seat and stood, and the whole crowd rose almost as one. It was a tremendous moment when the whole staff, the whole family of Prison Fellowship, stood with me even as I had led them into what really did imperil the ministry."

Prison Fellowship weathered the storm, but the breach between Colson and his old friend and mentor R. C. Sproul never healed. The two men and their ministries traveled separate paths from that time on. And there were more clouds on the horizon: within a year, another financial crisis, the second blow of a fiscal one-two punch, would drive the PF leadership literally to its knees and demonstrate anew the power of God's grace.

In ECT Colson had hoped to harness the power of separate Christian traditions to serve their common goal of evangelism. In spite of the backlash from some quarters, the joint statement was an encouraging step toward cooperation. (In years since, the group has issued historic statements on justification (1997) and scriptural interpretation (2002), and continues exploring ways to narrow the gap and improve the understanding between its two traditions.)

In 1995 Prison Fellowship had the chance to participate in an invitation-only financial program that offered 100 percent return on charity funds in six months. Originating in Philadelphia, the Foundation for New Era Philanthropy claimed to have lined up anonymous benefactors who would match contributions dollar for dollar. Its charismatic leader, John G. Bennett, Jr., kept the participation list exclusive while charities, hearing of New Era's incredible opportunity, clamored to get in. Early contributors got double their money as promised and word spread through the nonprofit network like wildfire. Eventually two hundred charities invested more than three hundred fifty million dollars with New Era.

Based on past performance and the status of those recommending the move, the PF board leaned strongly in favor of investing half a million dollars in New Era. But as the discussion worked its way around the table Jack Eckerd said quietly, "If you do it you'll have to replace me." Continuing over the murmur that rippled through the room, he explained that he thought the deal didn't smell right. He was opposed.

Jack didn't run the risk of losing his board seat on principle.

According to PF tradition, his objection meant they wouldn't go forward. From the beginning Prison Fellowship has observed the practice of never having a divided board. All approvals are unanimous. If after all the talk is over one person feels in his heart that a motion before the board is wrong, precedent calls for the motion to be set aside.

Once Jack spoke up, others shared their doubts. Another board member, Ken Wessner, voiced his agreement with Jack. "If it's too good to be true, it probably is." Prison Fellowship held on to its half million.

In May 1995 after New Era suffered a cash crunch, an investigation revealed the whole operation as a Ponzi scheme: there were no anonymous benefactors. Early investors were paid their 100 percent return out of the contributions of later participants, who in turn were repaid with still later funds until the number of new contributors couldn't keep up with the promised results.

New Era mastermind John Bennett was eventually convicted of a host of charges including fraud, money laundering, and tax evasion, and sentenced to twelve years in federal prison. Most of the victimized charities got back eighty-five to ninety cents per dollar invested. Though they didn't contribute a nickel to New Era, Prison Fellowship saw their contribution level take a frightening nosedive. The public didn't take the time to sort out who had invested in what. All they knew was that charity contributions had been frittered away in a Ponzi scheme, and they weren't throwing good money after bad.

The Prison Fellowship fiscal year ends on June 30. Between the time of the New Era bombshell and the last week in June, contributions slowed to a trickle. For the first time ever, the ministry faced a year-end deficit. Chief financial officer Bob Anderson and president Tom Pratt told the board, "We're going in the hole." With the few days they had remaining the board tried everything it could think of to shore up the balance sheet and cover the shortfall, but by June 29 they were still a million dollars short. That day they met together, got down on their knees, and asked God for a miracle.

The next day Prison Fellowship received a phone call from a New York lawyer whose client, PF records later showed, had been a nominal contributor to the ministry. The man had just died, the lawyer said, and had left Prison Fellowship a million dollars. Bob Anderson posted the amount that day, the last day of the fiscal year, and the ministry ended in the black by a hair. No one who knelt in prayer the day before had any doubt that God was watching over them with a special grace.

As the ministry continued to grow, there were opportunities that it declined because the board concluded they might steer them away from the ministry they felt God had called them to do. For example, in 1996 the Maclellan Foundation of Atlanta came to Chuck with an open-ended question: What could they do to support the Prison Fellowship worldview? They offered to fund a Christian think tank if Colson would run it. Tempting as the offer was, Colson declined, in part because he was just beginning work on a new book that he hoped would advance the Christian worldview from his twenty-five years of experience and study. A book had the potential to make a big cultural impact; Colson didn't want to give that up to spend his time issuing policy statements and research studies.

The book, written with Nancy Pearcy and published three years later, was *How Now Shall We Live?* It called Christians to look at their faith as something far more than Sunday morning church. Christianity, as Chuck had said in his speeches and radio broadcasts for years, was an all-encompassing worldview. Christians needed to present the gospel as a real-world solution to a culture of relativism and immorality. To do that, they needed to understand themselves as the vibrant force that Christianity was and how to explain and defend it in their everyday lives:

> The Church's singular failure in recent decades has been the failure to
> see Christianity as a life system, or worldview, that governs every area
> of existence. . . . We cannot answer the questions our children bring
> home from school, so we are incapable of preparing them to meet the

challenges they face. . . . We cannot explain to our friends and neighbors why we believe, and we often cannot defend our faith. And we do not know how to organize our lives correctly.

Who are we and where did we come from? What's wrong with the world? How can it be fixed? For answers Colson turned to his great heroes of the faith—Calvin, Kuyper, Lewis, and Schaeffer—then presented the solutions in everyday, nontheological language. *How Now Shall We Live?* became one of Colson's best-selling books and led to a series of related study guides and other publications.

Successful as it was, royalties from this latest book weren't enough to insulate Prison Fellowship from the consequences of the "dot-com recession" of 2001. With companies across the country in financial straits and the stock market sinking, friends of the ministry had less money to give. "The number of donors didn't change," Tom Pratt recalled, "the amounts changed." More worrisome was the fact that pledges made within the year from reliable donors were considered as income; when pledges went unhonored, the budget went out the window.

The budget for fiscal 1999–2000 was 53.5 million dollars, comfortably under projected income. But millions in contributions disappeared when the dot-com bubble burst, leaving Prison Fellowship in the red for the first time ever. Next year's budget was trimmed but, as Pratt observed, "We couldn't get the ministry down fast enough and gracefully enough."

The budget stabilized at last and the ministry got back on firm financial footing. Doing so required some hard choices, including painful reductions in staff. In the middle of all this financial turmoil Prison Fellowship installed its sixth president, though the timing had nothing to do with fiscal matters. The leadership was in complete accord through the tough years, pulling together as one to carry the ministry safely out of its most significant financial setbacks. Chuck, Tom Pratt, and the board had in fact spent four years crafting a plan

to find a servant leader to succeed Tom and for the first time to shoulder a significant share of Chuck's high-profile speaking and fund-raising
responsibilities.

Chuck had commissioned a transition committee in 1991 headed by
Kent Wessner, chairman of Service Master Corporation, whose death
from cancer was a great loss to the ministry as well as a personal loss
to many of the board members. In 1998 the transition committee
became the search committee whose charge was to find a successor.
The final selection of a man to lead Prison Fellowship into the third
millennium of Christianity was a long time coming, but, Chuck said, it
was "one of the great stories of God's providence."

One person Chuck was interested in for the job was Mark Earley,
attorney general for the state of Virginia, who had previously served
ten years in the state senate. A religion major at William and Mary,
Earley had spent a year in campus ministry with the Navigators, then
served two years at the University of the Philippines before returning
to the U.S. for a law degree. His experience overseas had convinced
him that Christians had a responsibility to be involved in their communities, their government, and their institutions to preserve the free-
doms God had given them. He believed law would give him a means to
do that through public policy or public service work.

In 2000, Dois Rosser contacted Mark on behalf of the board and
invited him to consider taking over the leadership of Prison
Fellowship. Mark felt God was using him best as Virginia's attorney
general and removed his name as a candidate for the PF position.

The committee continued its work, considering literally dozens of
prospects and talking with a number of them. "We talked to executives
of major corporations, prominent ministry leaders, senators, you name
it," David Cauwels recalled. Chuck Colson saw the hand of Providence
plainly in a conversation he had with PF executive Alan Terwilleger on
a bus during a Prison Fellowship event in California. They were dis-
cussing one prime candidate for the job when a passenger sitting

behind them said, "You're not thinking of this fellow are you?" then revealed some disturbing details about the person that put him out of the running. "The chances of that happening by coincidence are very remote," Colson noted.

One prospect for the job seemed the best fit, and after three years of work the search committee authorized the board to make him an offer. But the board hesitated. In the end, they decided not to move forward for the moment.

In 2001 Mark Earley resigned his office as attorney general to run for governor of Virginia. He lost the election by 1.5 percent. A few days after the defeat, Chuck called and asked Mark if he'd be willing to talk again. When he agreed, Chuck, Dave Cauwels, and other board members met with Earley in Richmond a few days before Christmas. With his experience and connections in government, Mark had the prospect of a very successful and lucrative career. Yet he agreed to pray with his wife, Cynthia, about the prospect of joining Prison Fellowship. Chuck later invited the two of them to meet with PF officers.

In a matter of days the search committee, the executive committee, and the full board all met by phone to consider Mark Earley as their new president. All three votes were unanimous, and Mark assumed his new post on February 1, 2002.

Why did Chuck identify this man as his successor years before? What about him made the board so comfortable so fast after years of searching? Dave Cauwels, who personally met with every serious prospect for the position, said a combination of attributes convinced them that Earley was the right choice.

First, "he had a heart after God." He wasn't interested in the job at first, but he listened to God's calling. "He could have done anything" he wanted to do, but he wasn't worried about his future or his career or his family. He was worried about being obedient to God's will.

Second, he wasn't a Chuck Colson clone. Rather he was the man God wanted to pick up where Chuck and Tom left off. Third, he was a

Navigator who knew about using God's Word to lead and train others. Fourth, as a former prosecutor and attorney general, he knew first-hand about the legal system, prisons, and prisoners.

With the new leadership in place, Chuck looked forward to less travel and more time to write. "I've had to learn how to back off," he admitted. He believes Mark's management style is a good change from his own. He is by his own admission a "type A-plus, while Mark is more of an encourager." The transition, in Chuck's estimation, has been "tremendous."

By the year 2000, Prison Fellowship had outgrown the beautiful and convenient Reston campus that had once seemed so spacious. Prison Fellowship International had once again been squeezed out to another location, as had various other components of the ministry. The board considered adding on to the Reston complex, but the cost projections were astronomical. As they had more than fifteen years before, PF needed the room, wanted to stay in northern Virginia, but couldn't imagine where the money would come from.

David Cauwels led the charge once more in looking for a new home. The board prayed about what the Lord would have them do. Cauwels recalled, "We couldn't raise the money for a new office, so finally five or six of us went in and paid for a piece of property ourselves."

Once those donors got the ball rolling, a handful of generous and visionary friends gave the money for a new building complex that allowed the whole ministry to be under one roof again for the first time in years—with room to spare. The main office was an elegant brick and glass building five stories high, surrounded by trees, combining modern lines with traditional colonial details. In front of it stood a separate guesthouse for official visitors and distinguished guests. And all for millions less than it would have cost to remodel the Reston campus.

Prison Fellowship moved onto the new property the week after Christmas 2004. Walking through the beautifully landscaped grounds, a visitor has a hard time imagining a cramped basement and desks made from surplus doors.

CHAPTER 16

Running the Race

For every prisoner who was a Christian or became one through Prison Fellowship there were many more—agnostics, atheists, Muslims, members of other religious groups and cults—who never heard of the ministry. PF programs went through the chaplain, but only an average of about 10 percent of the general prison population regularly attends chapel activities. That meant that for all Prison Fellowship was doing to reach inmates, 90 percent of them weren't getting the message.

The first big breakthrough in reaching the general population came in 1990 with the launch of *Inside Journal*, a newspaper written for the prison population. Its stories covered everything from profiles of famous ex-cons to how to order a meal in a restaurant, and how to dress for a job interview. Every issue had features written by inmates, letters to the editor, and other regular columns. In five years *Inside Journal* was distributed free in every state and federal prison in the country.

The most radical new way of reaching out to the prison population at large took root at a PF staff devotional in 1992. The guest speaker that day was Aaron Johnson, head of the North Carolina prison system and its ninety-four correctional facilities. Claude Rhea, a lawyer from

Alpharetta, Georgia, who spent eighteen years with Prison Fellowship, was at that meeting.

Aaron Johnson knew of Prison Fellowship's success in reducing recidivism and in-prison violence. He had come to welcome them into the entire state prison system. "I come as the man from Macedonia," Rhea recalled Johnson saying—referring to Paul's dream in Acts 16 when a Macedonian man pled with Paul and his companions to come and preach in his country (when Paul and others did so, they established the first Christian community in Europe)—"The prison doors are open to you."

PF leaders in the room looked around at each other with a combination of elation and concern. God had opened this door when they could least manage to walk through it. Beginning the year before, a nationwide recession had forced Prison Fellowship to tighten its belt. Donations were down, income projections were in tatters, and the ministry was in the middle of laying off employees. How could they possibly mount any sort of new program to make an impact on ninety-four prisons?

Tom Pratt believed the opportunity was too important to pass up. Specifically, the idea in North Carolina was to touch the lives of prisoners who kept their distance from the chaplain and had no interest in Christianity. Instead of Bible studies and hymn singing in the chapel, this program would be staged in the gym or out on the prison yard, with contemporary music, appearances by sports personalities, and other entertainment leading up to a gospel presentation. Every prisoner would know about the event and have a chance to take part, not just the chapel regulars. But even with thousands of local volunteers doing the heavy lifting, taking a show like that to ninety-four prisons would cost a million dollars or more. Yet Pratt believed the ministry somehow had to step through this door that the Lord had opened. With a team made up of Whitney Kunniholm, Myles Fish, and Richard Payne, Tom started planning, confident that God would provide.

Chuck talked with Hugh Maclellan, one of the most generous contributors to PF over the years, and floated the idea of responding to the

North Carolina challenge. Maclellan saw the value of the opportunity; moreover he saw the risk of letting a tight budget and layoffs bring an aura of defeat and timidity to the ministry. The Maclellan Foundation gave $1.5 million for the North Carolina outreach.

They christened the program Project Macedonia, a combination of music, testimony, and preaching directed at the majority of prisoners who weren't professing Christians. The festivities began with high-energy music to help gather the crowd and generate an uplifting atmosphere. Next there was Christian testimony from men that prisoners could identify with and who were respected within the prison culture. Not chaplains or preachers, not even Prison Fellowship representatives, but men who would rank high in the prison pecking order. The first show featured a demonstration by a former Mr. Universe. Prisoners respect physical power, and he commanded their attention right away. There were entertainers including Sherman Andrus, member of the Grammy Award–winning Imperials gospel group. And Chuck and others preached the gospel of Christ.

Project Macedonia dramatically improved the non-Christian prisoners' interest in Prison Fellowship. Seventy-five percent of the prison population came to the inaugural event. With several teams touring simultaneously, they covered all ninety-four North Carolina prisons in ten days. The next year, the Lowell Berry Foundation gave three hundred thousand dollars to take the idea to other prisons. Newly named Starting Line, then later Operation Starting Line, the program quickly expanded to other states.

Building on the encouraging response to pop culture plus Bible-based Christian teaching, Prison Fellowship partnered in the fall of 1994 with Grammy and Dove Award–winning Christian singer and songwriter Steven Curtis Chapman during his "Heaven in the Real World" tour. Chapman also spread the word during his tour performances about Angel Tree and other Prison Fellowship programs, plus the need for volunteers to expand them. He connected with a new generation of believers that Prison Fellowship had never reached before. Ultimately fifty thousand concertgoers and thirty-one hundred churches contacted Prison Fellowship as a result of Chapman's concert appeals.

Operation Starting Line (OSL) welcomed a variety of ministry partners to share in the work. By 2000 OSL was planning twelve tours a year, some including video messages from Billy Graham, others followed by a showing of the Campus Crusade for Christ *Jesus* film. In addition to the Billy Graham Evangelistic Association and Campus Crusade, the ministry's OSL partners by that time included the Navigators, Walk Through the Bible, Promise Keepers, Samaritan's Purse, the National Black Evangelical Association, and a host of other organizations.

The Navigators, Walk Through the Bible, and Prison Fellowship provided discipling follow-up, with volunteers committing to a year of aftercare. Prison personnel volunteered their time too for OSL. Security staff often came in during their weekends off in order to process the large number of visitors in and out and to monitor big gatherings of inmates. Once they saw how Operation Starting Line improved offenders' attitudes, they went out of their way to help events run smoothly.

Bringing musicians, speakers, audio/video equipment, lights, and busloads of volunteers inside a prison is a challenging task. Since no two prisons and no two prison staffs are the same, no two OSL presentations are prepared and staged the same. Misfires are bound to occur, one of which happened in the summer of 2001 at the notorious Rikers Island prison complex in New York, home to 14,500 prisoners in ten different institutions.

Problems began days before the scheduled event with an escape attempt, which brought on extra security precautions. Thirty OSL volunteers had their admissions granted, then revoked, then reconsidered, then revoked again. Eventually seventeen people got in. The day of the event, one member of the group had to get off the bus and take a taxi back to the hotel for ID badges that were left behind.

The gym where some events were staged had terrible acoustics; the program there started an hour late with twenty bored men attending.

Sixty eventually showed up, but were loud and rude, interrupting the show. A volunteer got violently ill; afternoon events were cancelled. And that was only the first day. Over the next two days, a singer fell and injured his knee, the sound crew were locked out of their hotel, and an amp exploded during a performance. Prisoners booed, cussed, and walked out en masse.

And yet God planted promising seeds. A transvestite delivering drugs to his "husband" stopped to check out the presentation and became a Christian. Some of the rude booing audience members had a change of heart later on. And volunteers handed out five thousand Bibles and seventy-five hundred Bible study booklets. Even in the midst of seeming frustration and failure, God's light shone through.

For more than twenty-five years, Chuck Colson had spent Easter Sunday in prison, preaching to inmates on that most important day on the Christian calendar, celebrating the resurrection of Christ. In 2005 he made his Easter visit as part of an Operation Starting Line program. A look behind the scenes during that weekend yields a representative taste both of Colson's thousands of prison visits and of what goes into planning and staging a successful OSL event. It is a microcosm of Prison Fellowship in action today.

On Good Friday evening 2005, a motel meeting room in suburban Charleston, South Carolina, buzzed with activity. The crowd chatted excitedly, some of them among old friends and others surrounded by newcomers. They had arrived throughout the afternoon from cities across the country, united by their passion to share the love of Christ with prisoners on the holiest weekend of the year. Some were college age, others retired, and they represented different ethnic groups with a range of regional accents. Some of them were already wearing their Easter-purple Operation Starting Line golf shirts. In only a few hours, all of them would have them on. It's how the prison staff would tell them from the inmates.

The din of voices tapered off to a polite rustle as an attractive and friendly-looking woman named Leslie Kent stood up at the front of the room. She was there both to clarify the logistics of getting two busloads of visitors into and out of three state prisons in thirty-six hours, and to remind the roomful of volunteers why they were there: to take greetings, encouragement, and the story of God's promise fulfilled through the Resurrection to South Carolina inmates. They were going to bring a sense of God's presence to the place, but, she added, "We don't take God behind the wall. He's already there."

Some of those listening were veterans of dozens of prison visits while others had never been behind bars before. Leslie told them not to worry about what they would say. "Be open; be yourself; don't preach or push; be a good listener." Another point was not to expect results on the spot or even soon. The Lord works on His own time.

The 2005 prison population in South Carolina is 76 percent black and 85 percent male. There are twenty-two thousand prisoners in the system, with thirteen thousand added and twelve thousand released every year. That means more than half of the state's prison population is turned back into the cities, towns, neighborhoods, and farms of South Carolina every year. As in all the other states, today's prisoners are tomorrow's neighbors. But on average the prison experience is overwhelmingly bad, not good. "Prisoners," Leslie continued, "build walls around themselves out of a sense of self-preservation." One of the best ways volunteers can chip away at that wall is simply to visit. They don't have to be theological scholars or have any of the answers to life's deep questions. They just have to be a friend in Christ.

Volunteers have booklets to hand out titled "Running the Race: A Bible-based 'Fitness Plan' for Your Life as a Christian." Interested inmates can use them to learn the fundamentals of the faith, see where the Bible teaches those fundamentals, request more information, or even sign up for a correspondence Bible course. There are no profound scholarly statements here. They're not necessary; God's promise of forgiveness and eternal life is as uncomplicated as it is universal.

In "Running the Race" the Good News is simply presented in seven statements with Bible verses to back them up: I am loved by God; I am forgiven by God; I have become a child of God; I am important to God; I am secure in God; I am God's creation; I am God's dwelling place. The prayer of acceptance on the last page is equally simple and complete:

> Dear Heavenly Father, I admit that I have messed up my life. I have sinned against You. Forgive my rebellion. I accept the death of Jesus on the cross for my sin. I surrender to You as the Lord of my life. Come into my life to live forever. I turn from my old way of living to follow Your way. Give me the power to live a new life in Christ. Thank You for loving me so much. I am forever grateful. In the name of Jesus I pray. Amen.

After a leisurely breakfast on Holy Saturday (the Saturday before Easter Sunday) the volunteers split into two teams and boarded separate buses. While one went to the Coastal Pre-Release Center, the other went to the MacDougall Correctional Institution. The program at MacDougall was outside in the yard, an open space of about twenty acres ringed by cellblocks and other buildings and enclosed by a tall wire fence. A temporary stage and sound system were set up on one end of the yard.

The Operation Starting Line program launched with a rousing welcome by the DJ-style master of ceremonies and a high-energy opening song by the Annie Moses Band. This rising Nashville group had three young siblings up front as a string trio, with Annie on violin, brother Alex on viola, and younger brother Benjamin on cello. Their dad, Bill, played electronic keyboards, while mom Robin sang backup vocals. A drummer and electric bass player rounded out the ensemble.

Young as the featured players were (Benjamin was underage, and OSL had to jump through various hoops to get him in as a visitor), they dug in with artistic fire and professional precision, with Annie jumping around the stage as she played, her long hair flying. The music from temporary speakers set up in the yard attracted a crowd. At the scheduled time perhaps two hundred men came outside to see what was going on. A few early arrivals drifted away from the stage and formed clusters with other men at the back of the yard, but most of them clapped and whistled enthusiastically. The first number brought hundreds more men pouring out of the cellblocks.

Some came up front as far as the rules allow, fifty feet or so from the stage, and sat in rows on the short grass. On the sides of the stage, men stood in groups and listened. In the middle distance, a few inmates sat on wooden benches and took it all in.

After two or three songs the Annie Moses Band got a rousing round of applause as they turned the stage over to a personality who plenty of the audience could identify with. He was black, and his muscular build, battered face, and misshapen smile identified him as a pro boxer. He introduced himself as Marvis Frazier, son of the legendary 1970 world heavyweight champion Joe Frazier. I'm from Philadelphia," he said, "the city of brotherly love."—pause—"They hug you before they mug you." Waves of laughter rippled from the audience as Marvis continued.

He talked about the feeling of hopeless failure he had when his father saw him beaten in his only championship fight. Through the pain and humiliation of his defeat, Marvis's one thought was how disappointed his father must be and how desperately sad he was to have let him down and tarnished the Frazier name. He saw his father coming toward him through the crowd and braced himself for the words of disdain he knew were coming. But his father climbed into the ring, embraced his son, and said, "I love you, son, I love you." And that was all.

Most prisoners never had a father figure in the house; the image of a loving, forgiving father is alien to them. Marvis's story cast the relationship between God the Father and man in terms inmates understood and could respond to.

Other testimonies told of bad decisions made and consequences suffered. These were men like the men in their audience: they knew how to be tough, knew what it was like to have their freedom taken away. Because they had a shared history, the inmates took notice.

After some more music, PF president Mark Earley spoke to the men about what Prison Fellowship is and what they do. Mentioning the Angel Tree program made a connection with the audience. A rumble of recognition ran through the crowd as heads nodded. Most prisoners with children know about Angel Tree, though many don't know it was started more than twenty years ago by a PF staffer who was also an ex-offender.

Then Mark turned the program over to Chuck Colson who shared his testimony, talking of Watergate and the Nixon resignation, all of which happened before most of his audience was born. "I know I didn't have it as tough as you guys do in here," he acknowledged, "but I came back. And I'll keep coming back as long as God gives me the strength to do so." The yard erupted in cheers.

After another round of music the program ended and the men had a few minutes before lunch was ready. Chuck mingled among them, walking up to little knots of conversation and extending his hand—the same hand that had shaken the hands of numerous U.S. presidents, foreign dignitaries, and others of the most powerful men in the world— to grasp the hand of inmate after inmate.

At lunch around picnic tables in another area of the yard, Chuck sat with prisoners who took a table somewhat removed from the rest. Within minutes, the group was in animated conversation. The men were excited, intrigued, eager to speak, and eager to listen. They may never have heard of Watergate, but they knew when someone was interested in them.

Though the donated hamburgers were far from gourmet fare, the men devoured them gratefully, some of them eating two or three. At the end of the day, the visitors and inmates parted company reluctantly. Anyone who submitted the card in the "Running the Race" pamphlet was promised a follow-up contact.

The mood on the way back to the motel was enthusiastic, even exultant. God was surely at work behind bars in South Carolina.

Easter Sunday morning, the rain that threatened all the day before was falling in sheets as the first busload of volunteers gathered for breakfast before daylight. Yesterday the clouds kept things cool; but today they presided over a wet and gray landscape. By the time the bus left at 6:15, the sun had made little progress penetrating the gloom.

This first wave of volunteers was all men, the only visitors allowed on death row, the segregation block (the old "solitary confinement"), and the infirmary. The whole busload went through the security check together then split up inside. Mark and Chuck headed for death row, a small group went off to the infirmary, and the rest walked through long painted concrete hallways to the segregation block. In two spots where there were stairs, one of the visitors in a wheelchair had his chair backed up the steps one at a time by a guard.

The cellblock was several stories high, with a metal staircase rising up through the space to metal railings, concrete walkways, and rows of steel doors. Everything was freshly painted gray-green, the concrete walls textured by bright overhead lights. With little discussion the men divided into groups, one for each floor, and made their way forward.

The vista was a row of metal doors opening out into a tight three-story atrium with a gray metal staircase winding up through the middle of it. Above the doors was a second row on the second floor and then a third. The doors were close together along the atrium wall, each made of steel plate with a small rectangular opening at face level, though not big enough to stick a face through. In any case, the opening was filled by steel bars, which in turn were covered with a sliding Plexiglas panel locked shut. These were men sequestered from the general population for fighting, escape attempts, or other rules infractions. Though it's the "isolation" cell, each cubicle held two men—the consequences of overcrowding—and a state prison population that grows at the rate of a thousand a year. They left their lights off to keep from disturbing their sleeping cellmates. The only light came from florescent fixtures overhead in the hallways that hummed softly, their electronic buzz blending with the deeper whoosh of the heating vents.

Most inmates were still asleep. One stood at his little plastic-covered window with his hands on the bars.

"Hello," said a visitor. "Happy Easter."

He smiled. "Is it Easter? You lose track of the time in here." He was a young man, a boy with pale skin and a shock of blond hair. He had wire-rimmed glasses and wore a wrinkled T-shirt. "I'll be in here eighteen months." There was a short pause. "I tried to get out," he explained without prompting.

Daybreak through the narrow window behind him cast a leaden backlight that outlined the head behind the tiny window.

"What church are you all from?" None of the visitors had mentioned anything religious.

"We're not from any one church. We're from churches all over. We've come in to visit and to wish you Happy Easter."

"I used to go to church."

"You did?"

"Yep. Used to go. But now I'm here."

"Would you like me to pray for you?"

"Yeah."

And so the visitor obliged.

Walking by the last door in the row, almost under the stairway, a voice came past the window bars, through the Plexiglas and out of the dark.

"Hey!"

A visitor walked to the shielded opening. "Happy Easter."

"Happy Easter." The speaker was young and black and invisible. There seemed to be no window behind it, and no light went on. A dim outline formed away from the light that labored its way through the door opening. "What are you all doing here?"

"Just come to visit."

"Don't have many visitors. Got this letter from my wife, though. She writes pretty regular. Comes to see me. I'll be out in six months."

"That's great."

"It's tough, though. We've been having some problems. But she's writing." I hear the sound of paper unfolding. "I just got this one."

"That's great. Your wife is a brave lady. A faithful wife is a real blessing."

"We're having some problems, though. But I think we'll get through it. She says she's been to a seer. What do you think about that?"

"I don't think it's a good thing. I read that we're supposed to run away from false prophets. Nobody who reads cards or reads your hand can tell you what's in store for your life."

"No?"

"No. You need to be careful. Don't let somebody take God's place in directing your life and your wife's."

"That's something to think about."

"Good. Could we say a prayer for you and your wife?"

"Yeah, say a prayer. That'd be good."

"Hey, everybody else is gone. Time to leave." It was a guard. The visitor had been worried about what to say, how to talk to these imprisoned strangers, and the time had flown by. Now he was the last one out of isolation. He had some tracts about basic Christianity, but the slots in the doors where food trays were passed through were all shut and locked.

"Slide it under the door," a voice called out. He'd never thought of that, though he had wondered why he had these booklets if there was no way to deliver them.

"Let me have one!" came another voice.

"Here!"

"Me too!"

"Whatcha got there?"

He slid as many under doors as he could as he half walked, half jogged out of the wing. The exit door slid open. A final voice hollered out, "Bring some women next time."

The team reassembled in the gym where the temporary stage was set up because of the rain outside. Visitors were in bleachers on one side as prisoners milled around on the basketball court and filled bleachers on the opposite side. Chuck's wife, Patty, was there as were Chuck's son Christian and his family, who lived in town. It's a rare opportunity for them to see the man they know as husband, father, and grandpa in the role that has made him a world figure.

The Annie Moses Band filled the room with music and energy, then shared their Christian testimony. Inmates turned quiet and reflective at the story of Marvis Frazier. He has a quiet voice for such a powerful-looking man, and inmates leaned forward to take in every word. Mark and Chuck spoke in their turn. A few men from the infirmary were in the audience, half-reclining in wheelchairs, their emaciated bodies covered with thick layers of blankets. Their complexions were white, their cheeks hollow.

Chuck told his audience that Christ Himself was a prisoner, falsely accused by a friend-turned-snitch, strip searched and mocked by His guards, tortured and executed. They hadn't gone through anything worse as prisoners than He did. He was one of them. And the only person in history assured by Christ to have a place in heaven was the believing thief crucified beside him, to whom He said, "Today you will be with me in paradise" (Luke 23:43). That promise is true for all people everywhere, thief or not.

As the cheers subsided, Chuck and the male visitors mingled with the crowd; women were confined by regulations to their places on the bleachers. Smiles and laughter punctuated the room. Hands reached eagerly for the Bible study booklets volunteers handed out by the boxful, both English and Spanish editions.

Drained but somehow on an adrenaline high, the volunteers boarded their buses for the motel and then home. They had bestowed what Oswald Chambers called the "tangible touch of Christ." At the first night briefing, Leslie Kent had said to them, "I pray that you'll never be the same again." To judge from comments and conversations that afternoon, her prayer was answered.

CHAPTER 17

Inner Change

The Brazilian judicial system has long been criticized for inefficiency, incidents of political favoritism, and widespread corruption; however, proposals for reform have been mired in controversy. Within the nation's prisons, harsh and overcrowded conditions have often incited mass escape attempts, rebellions, and riots, during which many prisoners have been killed."

This brief statement from the Encyclopaedia Britannica entry for Brazil only hints at the horrific conditions common in the prisons of Latin America's largest nation. Before constitutional reforms ended presidential rule by decree in 1988, conditions were worse. Then even more innocent people were subject to the inhuman treatment and primitive facilities of the system there. Guards were often brutal, and inmate-against-inmate violence was rampant; many prisons had no running water, no indoor toilets, and teemed with lice and vermin. Medical care was haphazard, meaningful spiritual nurturing almost nonexistent. And yet Brazil supplied Prison Fellowship with the template for what became their most inclusive, most expensive, most successful, and in some ways most controversial program ever, InnerChange Freedom Initiative (IFI).

In 1974 a Brazilian group of Catholic laymen called the Association for the Protection of the Convicted took control of Humaita Prison in Sao Jose dos Campos. According to Prison Fellowship's description, the facility adopted "a completely faith-based approach to all aspects of prison administration, security, and programming." Every aspect of operation became solely the responsibility of Christian community volunteers, with a bare minimum of government staff. The volunteers in turn passed the responsibility on to the inmates, along with Christian education in how to manage themselves.

Twenty years later, in 1994, Humaita had become a center of Christian teaching and mentoring, with Bible studies, life skills lessons, and job training foremost in the daily activities. Religious symbols were everywhere and inmates went to chapel daily. The former torture chamber was painted, equipped with a cross, and used for prayer. Two staff members supervised a population of 750. When men served their time and got out, they stayed out. The average annual recidivism rate over twenty years was 4 percent. The 1994 rate in the United States was 62.5 percent of ex-inmates rearrested within three years of release.

In the example of Humaita, Chuck Colson, Tom Pratt, and the rest of the Prison Fellowship leadership team saw a way to combine a full range of ministry programs under one roof, replacing a weekend seminar with a full immersion program that not only taught Christian precepts, but modeled Christian living and a Christian worldview every waking minute.

Their early enthusiasm was tempered by the knowledge they would face a battle in the United States over the issue of separation of church and state. Skirmishes flared up from time to time as it was, but a move so bold was bound to attract strong opposition. Years before he launched the IFI project, Chuck was a guest on conservative commentator William F. Buckley's TV show, *Firing Line*, and spoke for the first time about Humaita. He described their Christian approach and the mentoring of prisoners by Christian families, then compared the re-arrest rates of that prison with the American average, which was more than fifteen times higher.

Chuck later recalled, "During a break, I turned to the head of the Prison Project of the ACLU, who was another guest on the show, and asked what he would do if we tried to start a program like Humaita in the U.S. He said, 'I'd sue you, of course.'"

Not long before, Prison Fellowship board member, benefactor, and drugstore founder Jack Eckerd wrote a guest editorial for *Jubilee* bemoaning the money spent on correctional facilities and policies that were demonstrably useless.

> The average offender entering prison is twenty-five to twenty-nine years old, male, drug- or alcohol-dependent, functionally illiterate, with virtually no job history and low self-esteem. The sad fact is that he most likely will leave prison still drug-dependent and unemployable after years of idleness. He will have little hope of becoming a productive, tax-paying citizen. For all this, taxpayers pay $30,000 each year he spends behind bars. . . . We cannot fool ourselves into thinking barbed wire and empty hours are a recipe for rehabilitation.

As Prison Fellowship struggled to find a way to implement the Humaita model while respecting non-Christian prisoners' First Amendment rights, Eckerd offered to finance a study of the issue. The ministry hesitated to push forward with any sort of plan that would attract distracting and expensive legal challenges. Politically and legally, it seemed untenable.

The first hint of traction came during a meeting with the legal counsel to Alabama Governor Fob James. Chuck, PF staffer Claude

Rhea, the head of the Alabama prison system and others met in Montgomery, near Maxwell Air Force Base where Colson had once been a prisoner. The group decided to travel to Brazil and see Humaita for themselves. Governor James, who strongly opposed the growing judicial trend toward stripping symbols and statements of faith from public life, saw in Humaita an example that could transform Alabama's prison system and save millions of tax dollars.

Two events sent the Humaita study in a new direction. First, the Alabama Ethics Commission ruled that Governor James could not use state funds to travel to Brazil to look at a Christian prison. Second, the chairman of the Texas Board of Criminal Justice, Carroll Vance, got wind of the Humaita story and asked to take the trip along with PF. If there was going to be a breakthrough in prison management, Vance wanted to be sure not to let Alabama beat Texas to the mark.

When Alabama was forced to pull out, Vance and Colson led the trip. What Vance saw astonished him: prisons run according to Christian principles truly did rehabilitate criminals. They appealed to the heart, nurturing humility, accountability, and responsibility. And they worked wonders in a country where the average rearrest rate of 84 percent was even higher than in the U.S.

"Do you want to know if Christ is real?" Chuck asked. "Look at these results."

Vance returned to Texas ready to do whatever it took to launch a Humaita-based program in his state. Governor George W. Bush completely supported the idea. Like Colson, they feared a preemptive strike from the ACLU. Vance asked the governor to have the state attorney general do what he could to keep the ACLU at bay long enough for them to draft a request for proposal on a prison management contract that would pass constitutional muster.

The final RFP was open to proponents of any faith, or no faith at all, who were willing to set up a total immersion life skills program for volunteer participants. No lawsuits were filed; Prison Fellowship won the contract and went to work developing America's first-ever full-time in-prison Christian environment at the state correctional facility outside Sugar Land, near Houston. In 1997 Governor Bush came to visit and agreed that the program was a tremendous success. At the end of his visit the governor locked arms in a circle with inmates and joined in singing "Amazing Grace" with them.

Thanks to work behind the scenes from PF cofounder Al Quie, Governor Jesse Ventura implemented IFI in Minnesota. Kansas and Iowa also set up programs, with others now in the planning stages. These programs are the greatest testament of all to the work of Prison Fellowship and the grace of Christ in changing the hearts of prisoners, giving hope, stability, success, and forgiveness they never had before.

Anyone who has ever been in prison as an inmate, visitor, or staff member is likely to react to his first IFI encounter with slack-jawed astonishment. The IFI program at Newton Correctional Facility near Newton, Iowa, fairly represents the rest. One cellblock is a dedicated IFI area; every prisoner living there is a volunteer participant in the program. Non-Christians are welcome, but the program is overtly and unapologetically Christian.

Inside the cellblock there is no sense of fear, no sexual tension, no violence. In four days on the grounds a visitor hears not one word of profanity. The surroundings are clean, and every inmate is busy. Blacks, whites, and Hispanics work together, eat together, and spend free time together—a situation virtually unheard of in a prison environment. They greet a stranger with a welcome, a handshake, and a steady gaze. In four days, a visitor never once opens a door. There's always someone waiting to do it for him.

Inmates from the general prison population who volunteer for IFI have an interview with Dan Kingery, the program director. Applicants have to have at least eighteen months left on their sentence, must qualify for a medium security classification, and be functionally literate. They can't have a history of violent behavior or mental instability.

Sexual offenders have to have completed required treatment. Offenders come initially to IFI for all sorts of reasons. Out of a recent class, one came because he lost a bet. He ended up wanting to stay in the program. Another participant heard that IFI prisoners had a big-screen TV. In reality, IFI participants give up television altogether. This is a huge sacrifice in a place where watching TV is one of very few ways to pass the time. Though the participant found no big screen, he decided to stay as well. Yet another came at first in order to work in the computer lab. The atmosphere of friendship and support made him want to continue.

Inmates who come to an IFI interview thinking the Christian program gives them more privileges soon learn the opposite is true. In addition to no TV, IFI members have to give up all pornography, reduce their precious visiting time, and stick to a demanding daily schedule. The same schedule keeps them from most of the best prison job assignments. Mandatory small group devotionals begin at six in the morning, five days a week, and participants can't be late. Evening classes run until eight fifteen every weeknight. There's an informal worship service every afternoon at three o'clock, plus church on Sunday morning. The men have to keep devotion logs and turn in their class work on time. "Some inmates come in thinking they can fake it," program director Kingery noted. "They want to be part of this environment, and so they think they can pretend to be interested in the classes. What they learn after a while is that you can't fake it for eighteen months."

After a thirty-day orientation period, inmates accepted into the program who want to continue spend twelve months in Phase 1, which includes a full day of devotionals, Bible study, education classes, and job training or work on the prison grounds. Like all IFI students, they have access to an IFI computer lab, library, and classrooms. Classes of twenty to forty men go through Phase 1 together under a biblical counselor who is an IFI staff member. There are usually at least half a dozen classes under way at once, each at a different point in their twelve-month cycle.

Phase 2 takes place the last six months of a participant's sentence. Devotionals and worship time are the same as in Phase 1, but instead of classroom time inmates ramp up their school or work hours. Also in Phase 2, each man is matched with a volunteer Christian mentor who meets with him weekly. He is a friend and guide who encourages the inmate to live a Christian life through the end of his sentence and keeps meeting and working with him for a year after his release. Phase 2 men also meet with aftercare counselors who help set up housing, employment, and a welcoming church for the inmate as soon as he is released.

Phase 3 extends for a year beyond the release date. Inmates who have served their time are tempted by old friends and old ways when they get out. As one seasoned counselor put it, "I can tell you who's going to make it on the outside by who picks them up at the bus station. If it's the same old crowd they were running with before, their chances are slim." IFI follows each participant back to the outside through weekly meetings with his mentor and his aftercare counselor, and encourages weekly church attendance, Bible study, and Alcoholics Anonymous/Narcotics Anonymous meetings as necessary.

According to a University of Pennsylvania study, IFI cuts the reincarceration rate for ex-offenders who've been out of prison for two years by almost two-thirds. But it's expensive: each of the IFI programs, up and running, costs six hundred thousand dollars per year. And despite the track record, some prison authorities want nothing to do with it. It means more trouble for them, and some see it as a first step toward privatization of prisons, which would put them out of a job.

InnerChange Freedom Initiative is the ultimate expression of the Prison Fellowship worldview connecting morality and crime. The ministry has brought Christian standards into some of the darkest, most fearsome places in American society and transformed them into places of refuge, hope, and triumph. IFI cellblocks are today among the safest, cleanest, friendliest, most optimistic communities in the country.

Where every other solution has failed significantly to improve prison living conditions and reduce recidivism, IFI has succeeded repeatedly. And the ripple effect of these transformed ex-inmates dramatically extends their influence. Instead of the repeat offenders they were statistically destined to be, they become wage earners, taxpayers, family providers, community leaders, and examples and mentors to others they touch along the way. Those in turn influence a new circle of men and women. And the work of IFI continues, ring after concentric ring, enriching lives of people who have never even heard of it.

For all the difference IFI inmates make once they're released, some of the richest spiritual journeys have been taken by men who may spend the rest of their lives in prison. Let's meet a few of them.

CHAPTER 18

James, Ron, and Matthew

Introducing himself to a visitor, James Corder is soft-spoken and polite, open and cordial, almost passive. A shock of straight blond hair falls down over his glasses. He is tall, broad-shouldered, and healthy looking, though his skin is pale from the short, dim days of midwinter in Iowa. While he looks like he's college age, or maybe in graduate school, he's actually in his mid-thirties. He's an ace with computers, but he didn't even graduate with his high school class.

When he was seventeen, James murdered his stepmother with a butcher knife and set her house on fire. He was convicted of first-degree murder and sentenced to life in prison without possibility of parole. He's been in prison seventeen years, half his life; if he lives to an average old age he'll die in prison around 2050.

His home for the last five years has been the Newton Correctional Facility, an island of floodlights in an ocean of rolling farmland three miles from Newton, Iowa, home of Maytag appliances and world-class blue cheese. Two tall wire fences encircle the compound, each topped with the neatly coiled razor wire, specially designed and installed to disembowel anyone trying to climb over it. This innovation, along with high-tech motion detectors and video cameras, has made traditional masonry walls and watchtowers obsolete. Guards armed with pistols and shotguns patrol the outer perimeter in pickup trucks. Guards inside carry no firearms, lest one of them fall into the wrong hands.

Prisoners sentenced to life without parole tend to be peacemakers in the tense, violent world behind bars. They expect it to be home to them for the rest of their lives, so they want to keep the commotion down, keep the gang fights and thefts and murders to a minimum. James didn't start out as a peacemaker, and he has the scars to prove it. Fearful though he was at first, he didn't have to do much fighting even early in his sentence. A first-degree murder conviction put him at the top of the prison social order. He was obviously unpredictable, and had nothing more to lose no matter what he did to anybody. Other inmates left him alone.

The overwhelming feeling in prison, James said, is one of loneliness, with each inmate huddled in his own world, his connection to familiar things on the outside broken. "The most intense feeling is a sense of separation from the society I lived in," he said. "When those doors closed behind me and I started the admitting process, suddenly everything I knew was changed. In prison you're separated from everything you know. That is the punishment."

That overwhelming loneliness comes in spite of a complete lack of privacy. "You can be strip searched any time," he explained. "That's the most degrading part of prison life. They take you out and strip all your clothes off and look you over, up and down. Luckily most times they don't do what's called a cavity search, like when they first put you in jail and check for drugs and weapons. But it's still degrading."

James went through various rehabilitation classes. Some inmates go through them hoping to shorten their sentence or impress the parole board. With no chance at parole, James took classes because the prison administration told him to. He shares most prisoners' opinion that the classes are well-intentioned but practically useless.

Prison bureaucracy loves programs. They get one going and then they start requiring it. When I first came to prison [in a different facility], I went to education programs and got my high school diploma. I took parenting classes, anger management. Once in a while someone will say, "Hey, let's start a computer class so people will have a skill when they get out," but they don't look at the underlying problem of a man still wanting to commit a crime.

OK, you get a certificate. Just like Pavlov's dogs you can learn to do what you need to do to move forward. You feel like a circus animal jumping through hoops. But then you get out and you swing by the bar, the crack house, whatever. Parenting classes aren't going to help you. People in corrections know it's not working, but they say there's nothing else.

For thirteen years there was nothing else for James. He did his time day by day, collected his course certificates, and watched TV, the "babysitter" the prison administration "hands out like candy," he said, "because when you're watching TV you're not beating up on Joe or John."

One day he heard that another unit at Newton needed somebody to help run their computer lab. When his transfer there was approved, that's where he found the "something else" that transformed his life.

The unit is one of a handful across the country that makes up the InnerChange Freedom Initiative. Inmates who volunteer and who qualify for the program spend eighteen months in the "God pod," separated from the general prison population and subject to special rules.

"I'm no longer doing what I used to do, and that's thinking about myself first," James continued. "In my criminal mode I thought like a child. That's the way we come to prison—'Society owes us!' No, society doesn't owe us, we need to change. Proverbs says the wicked seek to ensnare the righteous, yet we end in folly.

"I was still lying about my crime, saying I didn't commit it. I lied about it for twelve years. I realized I was trifling with God and I got nervous. What I saw around me [in IFI] was good, right, just. But to walk with Christ I'd have to confess. Now I can say it. I murdered my stepmother. But that wasn't the end. I had to tell my family what I did, the living victims.

"I lied to my mom and dad and all the rest of the family who supported me through the whole ordeal. After I was baptized in prison, I started saying Christ was in charge and I had to change. My biggest fear was telling my parents, grandparents, aunts, uncles, cousins. That's why I lied in the first place. I wasn't afraid of the state, I was afraid of them.

"I wrote a letter to my stepmother's brother. Whether he reads it or not, God's in charge. In the past my goal in writing would have been to somehow get out of prison. Now it's to help him. I now can offer something to society I couldn't offer when I came to prison. I had nothing society needed from me. Now I have the good work of the Lord to offer. I know I can add something to society now, and from what I see in the papers, I'm needed.

"No one changes his heart. God has to soften the heart. And then man has to be willing to have that heart change from stone to flesh. We pretty much want to harden our hearts; it's the natural reaction to everyday experience. My whole goal now is that everything I do serves God, and He can use that to glorify His kingdom."

Ron Gruber joined a motorcycle gang called the Sons of Silence when he was fourteen. "I had a big empty spot inside," he explained, and he thought the protection and sense of family in a gang would fill that emptiness. When they fought, the Sons of Silence brought violence to a new level of brutality with bricks, bottles, baseball bats, and whatever other crude, destructive weapons were readily at hand.

Before long Ron looked every inch the part of a motorcycle gangster. He had long scraggly hair, a full beard that grew halfway down his chest, and arms covered with tattoos. In 1979 he was in prison. Reconnecting behind bars with members of the Sons of Silence, he was as feared as an inmate as he had been on the outside. Revenge and violence motivated and drove him. One guard in particular especially irritated him, and when he saw the guard, named Mapes, laughing as he padlocked a cell, Ron and his gang decided it was time to retaliate.

"We had said it was time to hurt this guy, and today is his day."

What Ron and his cohorts didn't know was that Mapes was following orders, padlocking a prisoner because he had homemade alcohol in his cell. The prisoner was drunk and he and Mapes were joking and laughing together at the situation. "Every time you have a party, someone comes along and ruins it!" All Ron, who was also drunk, heard was the laughing and thought the guard was making fun of the prisoner. The inmate mob attacked Mapes, grabbed his security buzzer and his keys, and started beating him. "We proceeded to bust his head wide open," Gruber recalled.

He was rescued before Ron could throw him over the third floor railing, but he still suffered a concussion, chipped teeth, bruised ribs, and a gash in his head requiring stitches. "He was a typical example of the worst people in prison," Mapes recalled later. "He was a nasty, filthy, broken person who preyed on people and victimized them. He lived only for the here and now: sex, drugs, and violence."

When Ron finished his prison term in 1982 he went right back to his old gang and his old ways. Twelve years later, his violent, angry life had gotten him in even worse trouble than before. When he learned he was being hunted not only by the state for murder but also by the FBI for racketeering, he stopped for the first time in his life and thought about the future.

"I went out into the woods for two weeks," he said, "to think about what I should do." He thought about the emptiness and purposelessness that had defined his life and led him to this point. "I didn't see any bright light or anything like that. But I felt God inside my heart. I saw

myself as I really was. I got down on my knees under the trees and con-
fessed everything I had ever done and asked Christ to forgive me. Then
I turned myself in to the FBI."

Ron was eventually assigned to the state penitentiary in Newton,
where he threw himself wholeheartedly into Christian service with all
the energy he had once spent on crime and violence. When a new warden came to Newton, the warden soon came to visit the cellblock where
volunteers participated in the Prison Fellowship IFI program, and
where Ron Gruber was known as a strong and dedicated prayer warrior.

The warden and the prisoner were almost face-to-face before they
recognized each other: the warden was former guard Terry Mapes,
whom Ron had tried to kill fifteen years before. Immediately Ron
extended his hand and said, "Mr. Mapes, I'm sorry. I'm sorry for all the
pain I've put in your life."

Warden Mapes stood for an instant looking at the outstretched
hand. "I swore I'd never do this," Mapes said, then grasped the hand
with a firm grip. "He shook my hand," the warden said. "He was a different man. Years in confinement hadn't changed him. What I saw
couldn't have happened without divine intervention."

Soon afterward, Ron encountered another former target of his
gang-era rage. Ken Lockhart, a businessman and friend of Prison
Fellowship, was touring the IFI cellblock and being introduced to
various inmates in the program. He was shaking hands with Ron
Gruber before he realized who he was. They had been in high school
together when Ken inadvertently dated Ron's brother's girlfriend.
Ron and his gang had vowed to kill Ken for this offense, and Ken
feared for years that they would make good on their threat. Only
when he read that the Gruber brothers were back in prison had he
completely relaxed.

When he realized whose hand he was shaking, Ron felt the hair on
the back of his neck stand up. Ron's response was to say, "I'm sorry for
what I did to you. I hope you will forgive me. I earned your anger and

hate because I worked 110 percent to earn it." The two had lunch together, and by the end of the meal they were embracing as friends.

"How do you really know there's a God?" asked Ron. "I was a soldier for Satan and the darkness, but through the blood of Jesus Christ I'm now a soldier for God and the light."

Matthew Santamagro looks far too young to have been in prison five times. He is too young. His first felony conviction came when he was eight. He has spent most of his life since then locked up somewhere. But now his life is transformed by the saving grace of Christ through Prison Fellowship.

Sitting in a prison office of the InnerChange Freedom Initiative, a program he currently devotes virtually every waking moment to, Matthew looked like an up-and-coming young movie star: thick blond hair, ice blue eyes, a firm jaw, and a bodybuilder physique. But the face was scarred from years of prison yard battles; his body was the result of endless hours in prison weight rooms trying to grow stronger than the thugs who threaten him.

Matthew has a remarkable testimony, and he tells it far more compellingly than anyone else could tell it for him. This is his story, in his own words:

"I was born and raised in New York. My mom was thirteen. Dad was fifteen, but he was never part of the picture. I was raised by my grandparents. Mom and I lived with them in a one-bedroom apartment. We didn't have much, but I learned I could have what I wanted if I just took it. I was eight years old the first time I had a felony. I graduated from stealing clothes at the mall to breaking into houses and stealing things I could sell. Then I stole cars, and it got worse after that. Stole a couple of guns and got caught with those. I went through the juvenile justice system until I was sixteen, then into the adult system.

"My first experience with adult corrections was Rikers Island, a

JAMES, RON, AND MATTHEW [213]

county jail that also housed state inmates. The first day I walked in there was probably the scariest day of my life. It was a place where they didn't really send young white kids and that's what I was: sixteen years old, 125 pounds, blond hair, and blue eyes. Thrown into the lion's den. I remember not getting to eat, having all my food taken from me by other inmates just because they could, and I couldn't do anything about it.

"I got my head split open for not giving somebody my shoes. But I lost my shoes anyway. Prison is a dog-eat-dog world. Only the strongest survive. Corrections officers are so overworked they can't do much. They come in every hour or two, but you just do whatever you can to make it. I avoided confrontation as long as I could. I wasn't at Rikers very long, five or six days, but it changed me as a person. Even though I was a bad kid, I still had innocence. The experience took that away from me.

"I started to get angry, started to get a little bit racist. Became anti-social. I didn't like my mom because she didn't come right in and get me out, and she let me go through all that stuff. That led to a pattern that got me incarcerated in four different states. Since the first time I went to prison, I've never stayed out more than three months. I got caught up in this trap of hopelessness. It seemed like the system didn't care about me when I got out. They just kicked you out the door and waited for you to get in trouble, then brought you back in again. I tried everything when I got out. I didn't really want to go to prison.

"I was always told I had a lot of potential. I tried going through all the treatments in prison; that didn't help. Last time I got out I was going to college full time and working full time. I think I tried to do too much and failed again. I really tried to do it on my own every time I got out. It blew up every single time.

"The first time I went to an adult prison was in Colorado. It wasn't so bad as the New York system. It was also very racially segregated. If you were white, you were only allowed to talk to white people. Blacks and Mexicans the same way. I couldn't sit down at the table with a black guy or a Mexican guy, or the higher ups in the Aryan Brotherhood would punish me—roll up to my cell and let you know you messed up and don't let it happen again.

"That was the first place I ever got seriously hurt in prison. I had a roommate who got into debt with some guys in the yard, and I got in a fight with some of them over a basketball game. I came out on top in that situation, so to clear his debt they said he had to take care of me when they locked down the cell that night. I remember laying in my bed with my eyes closed but seeing some movement. He was coming down with a knife trying to stab me in the throat. Luckily I got my arm up, and it just caught me in the arm. I got stabbed twice. It turned into a pretty messy thing.

"Reputation is extremely important in prison because it's kind of a world where the worse you are as a person the higher your elevation in prison society. If you're a murderer, you're top notch. You'd be like the millionaire actors and sports stars in society. If you have the reputation of not taking any crap and being a fighter and doing whatever you have to do, that's good. That's your goal in prison: you want to work your way up this status ladder so the higher you get, the less problems you have—even from the corrections officers. They'll even get to the point where they think, you know, *We don't want to mess with this guy.*

"I was also incarcerated in Arizona, and down there they make everybody do 85 percent of their number, so there's no reason to behave. There's no good time benefit except 15 percent, and at that point you don't care too much. You can do anything you want because there's no repercussions unless you hurt somebody bad enough to go back to court and get more time.

"Arizona prisons have an extreme drug problem: heroin, cocaine, serious drugs, not just the marijuana you see everyplace else. Basically, it all comes down to an officer who's looking to make more money somehow. That was one of our main ways of getting contraband into prisons—through officers. They could make two thousand dollars for one trip rather than whatever they earn in salary a week.

"I believe that secular treatment programs for the most part don't work 90 percent of the time. I've been through other drug treatments five, six, seven times and used drugs while I was in treatment the whole time. I've been through their criminal thinking and this and that. It's just not realistically applicable when you face a situation that leads to criminal behavior. So I've never found any secular treatment in prison that helped me even a little bit.

"Why does IFI work? We have to give up a lot to come here. In other prisons you can just do your time. You can lay down and watch TV and gamble and cuss and do whatever you want to do. They really don't care as long as you're not hurting people and starting a lot of trouble. To come here you actually have to give up your television, you give up your free time, you give up a lot of things.

"For me I realized this is my fifth time back in prison. I've tried everything, and I'm going to die in prison if I keep this up. I just came to the point in my life where I understood that I can't change on my own. I've tried everything. It's impossible. I can't do it. I couldn't think of any avenue that was left that I could try on my own and succeed. And I just heard about this place. And at that point it had a 92 percent success rate, and to me that was amazing.

"I didn't believe in God. I didn't have anything against it, it just wasn't in my upbringing. I said I don't care what they do to me; I just want to be part of that 92 percent that doesn't come back to prison. That was my only reason for coming here. When I got to IFI, I saw people that I'd been in prison with before, some pretty mean guys that had real bad histories. My first 'cellie' I had when I came here was a guy I had a fight with the last time I was in prison. Here I come to this unit and I go to the same cell with him! And I'm thinking, *Oh, here we go.* But as soon as I walked in, he smiled sort of a timid smile and said, 'You're probably the last person I expected to see here, but

I'm really glad you chose to come.' It's just something you don't hear in prison.

"I probably wasn't here ten minutes and I had fifty guys shaking my hand. Even some freaking me out a little bit trying to hug me. Everybody had these smiles on their faces. I was like, 'You guys get no TV, you can't play cards, you can't go out on the yard—what's wrong with you people?' At first I thought it was kind of a show they put on when new people came—let's just put on this show and lure them in a little bit. The longer I was here the more I realized, hey these people really are happy and they have a peace about them for some reason. I started to think, *I want what they have.* That's just what it came down to.

"So I said, 'Well, I'll listen to what they got to say because obviously there's something to this whole God thing. I've looked at the Bible before, but it was kind of all over the place, the weird sayings, and these stories.' My roommate sat down and asked me to pray with him that God would help me understand these things. I felt like I was talking to the wall and it was all really weird, but we started doing a little Bible study every night and it just all started to make sense.

"After a couple of months of that, I got a big hunger to learn more. It was like I had all these questions my whole life, and yet this book that was written anywhere from two to four thousand years ago was answering all these questions I had! I finally took a leap of faith and accepted Jesus. It was amazing what's happened since then. Last time I was in prison I had I don't know how many [disciplinary] reports. I was always in the hole or in a fight or walking around the yard with my chest pumped out like, 'Who wants to mess with me?' because I thought that's what it was all about. Since I've been here I've gotten in no trouble, the Lord's kind of given me a heart for people. Before I was really always all about me. I would use anybody, including friends and family, to get what I wanted. And now—it still amazes me sometimes— it's like God always puts someone in my path who needs help. My needs don't matter so much.

"The weight yard used to be my prime focus: *I've got to get bigger and stronger.* About two months ago I took six months off because I felt it was interfering. I wasn't able to spend time with other people like I wanted to. And God really blessed me here. He put me in some leadership positions. I clerk for the drug treatment class. I help those guys and pray with them and do a little sharing and fellowshipping with them.

"I finally reached this point where I get reviewed by the parole board in a couple more months and there's no anxiety there. I'm actually happy that I've been in prison five times and happy about my childhood and the abuse and everything else that happened along the way because I was so harsh—that was the only way God could get through to me, to break me down further and further, let me go through these trials to get to this point today.

"There's really no place I'd rather be than where I'm at right now. There's no anxiety about when I'm going to get out. There's just a peace and expectancy and waiting to see where God's going to use me and what kind of plans he has. It's actually really exciting. He's already putting things together for my release as far as ministry work down in Missouri. I already have a job waiting for me, a place to stay waiting for me. Helping with a halfway house if they get IFI started down there. All these things that a drug addict criminal with a bad attitude would never have dreamed of happening a couple of years ago.

"A lot of us feel forgotten when we get to prison. Families are so sick of it. Our so-called friends we had are sick of us. You get here and you get locked in this box every night just with you and your thoughts. A lot of us don't have family or friends out there anymore. It seems like nobody cares. Prison Fellowship really makes a difference. The volunteers that come in show you that they really care. They give up time with their own families. They share their lives with us, people they hardly know. Their faces light up, they run over and give us hugs. It gives us hope more than anything that, wow! we're not worthless, we're not rejects of society that everybody's forgotten about. It gave me hope that people do still care.

"The way I first understood God's love was to see it through other people. How do they love us? They tell us the sacrifice Jesus made for their lives, and they're willing to sacrifice out of love for us and love for God. They don't even consider it a sacrifice. They actually look forward to coming in each week, and it's great. I love nighttime curriculum when you just see these people coming across the yard. In a lot of prisons you don't get to see people. Visitors don't even get to walk into most prisons. Most places they'd never allow you to walk across the yard. The closest we'd ever get to someone other than a corrections officer or a counselor or another inmate would be through the glass wall in the visiting room. That makes you feel even more like an animal, when you can't have contact with another person. A couple of nights a week we have an eighty-year-old woman who walks across this yard by herself with not a fear about anything. She feels comfortable; she feels safe. The fact that someone like that could walk around inside a prison, that's just unheard of.

"I believe that God put a protection around this place because it's like no other prison anywhere. You can walk the yard and hear guys quoting Scriptures to each other. Christians are actually persecuted in most prisons: there are those guys who can't face reality, who need a crutch.

"We have a revival every week. There are usually about four hundred prisoners and fifty to one hundred citizens that come in and do a praise and worship service every Friday. It's open to the general population. It gets packed. It's great, and it's loud.

"Any problem you have, there are counselors who'll stop whatever they're doing. At any point in the day, you can find fifty people who'll be willing to pray with you. Compared to the prison system generally, it's like a Garden of Eden in here."

CHAPTER 19

The Next Chapter

W here, then, does this leave Prison Fellowship Ministries at the turn of Christianity's Third Millennium? In a position of strength and promise, poised to begin the next chapter of its history.

PRISON MINISTRY

The core of Prison Fellowship remains its in-prison seminars. Today more than twenty-three thousand ministry volunteers in every state lead more than two thousand seminars a year in evangelism, discipleship, leadership development, and Bible study with more than 2.2 million participants (many inmates participate in several different studies). PF matches more than five thousand volunteer mentors a year with prisoners to help strengthen their faith and prepare them for life on the outside. It helps churches develop reentry programs to support ex-prisoners as they are restored to society. The ministry also funds the Charles W. Colson Scholarship for ex-offenders to Wheaton College.

Operation Starting Line continues reaching out to nonreligious prisoners with remarkable success. More than eighty thousand inmates attended 136 OSL presentations in 2004.

InnerChange Freedom Initiative continues in Texas, Iowa, Kansas, and Minnesota, with several other states requesting programs. New IFI operations depend on regulatory approvals and on availability of Prison Fellowship funds. To date, more than nine hundred inmates have graduated from the program. Eighty-five percent are currently employed. More than four hundred ex-offenders have completed the post-release aftercare portion of IFI.

Angel Tree now includes a mentoring program, a summer camp, and a football camp to minister to children of prisoners throughout the year. In 2004 more than 12,700 churches provided Angel Tree Christmas gifts to more than 550,000 boys and girls, while nearly 500 churches helped send 10,600 children to summer camps. PF supporters Richard and Helen DeVos donated $1.1 million for camp scholarships.

Along with personal ministry PF sponsors a pen pal program, matching volunteers with more than 20,000 prisoners each year who request someone to write to them. It also publishes *Inside Journal* for inmates and distributes it to every prison in the country. A circulation of 375,000 makes it one of the most widely read Christian publications in America.

WILBERFORCE FORUM

This wide-ranging PF ministry reflects Colson's belief that restoring and justifying a Christian worldview is essential to prison reform. As a recent annual report explained, Wilberforce Forum "marshals various programs and resources to equip Christians to influence all major cultural institutions: churches, education, business, law, government, and media." Today the list includes:

BreakPoint—daily radio commentaries by Chuck Colson and Mark

Earley, broadcast daily to an estimated one million listeners. Transcripts are e-mailed daily to fifty-five thousand subscribers.

Justice Fellowship—advocating criminal justice reform based on restorative justice principles.

Centurions—a yearlong training program begun in 2004 consisting of reading, study, seminar assignments, and personal encouragement to a select group of Christian men and women volunteers, equipping them to model, teach, and defend a biblical worldview.

Publications and Curricula—print, online materials, and studies examining modern culture and ways to apply faith to all its aspects.

Capitol Hill Lecture Series—an annual eight-week series for congressional leaders and staff on applying a Christian worldview to public policy.

Public Policy Advocacy—efforts to shape legislation on criminal justice reform, freedom of religion, sanctity of life, and human rights.

PRISON FELLOWSHIP INTERNATIONAL

PFI now has chartered affiliates in 106 countries around the world. The seventh World Convocation, in Toronto in 2003, brought 800 representatives from 113 countries and a variety of Christian traditions together to promote restorative justice and prison reform throughout the globe. Chairman Mike Timmis and president Ron Nikkel have taken international outreach to new heights. Of Timmis, Chuck exclaimed, "He has clearly taken the ministry far beyond anything I could have done. He has boundless energy and enthusiasm." Chuck added, "What thrills me, and what I think is significant, is that I'm chairman of Prison Fellowship USA, and I'm a Southern Baptist; Mike Timmis is chairman of Prison Fellowship International, and he's a Roman Catholic. This is a tremendous witness around the world."

GOD'S INSEPARABLE COMMISSIONS

In the Prison Fellowship 2004 annual report, Chuck Colson sum-marized his position that reforming prisoners is futile without trans-forming the culture they came from.

God is working wonders inside the prisons. But most prisoners are released into a culture that no longer values the dignity of human life, which includes outcasts like ex-prisoners. Without help in society they're going to return to crime. So the Church has to be passionate about advocating justice and human dignity. We see the same lesson with Angel Tree. We're able to reach the prisoners' children and pre-sent the gospel, but just think how they are bombarded on all sides by a commercialized culture promoting promiscuity and permissiveness. Unless the culture can be reclaimed, much of our work will be in vain.

No, these two things go hand in hand, bringing the life-changing power of Jesus to those in need, and working for justice and righteousness in our society. In fact, the work we've done in the prisons over the years has given us enormous credibility to speak out on these worldview issues.

One issue Prison Fellowship has emphasized recently is protecting prisoners from sexual assault and rape. Colson described prison rape as "a hidden epidemic" suffered by three hundred thousand to six hundred thousand inmates a year. A study of Nebraska prisons found 22 percent of inmates acknowledged being pressured or forced into sex acts; 25 percent of this group said they were gang-raped. Justice Fellowship promoted the Prison Rape Elimination Act of 2003, which passed both houses of Congress with strong bipartisan support.

Looking ahead to that next chapter for Prison Fellowship Ministries, there's cause for cautious optimism. Incarceration rates for the youngest state and federal prisoners have dropped even as the overall prison population has risen because of mandatory sentencing guidelines. In September 2005, the Department of Justice reported that in 2003 there were 10 percent fewer eighteen- to nineteen-year-olds in prison than in 1995. Better still, there were 40 percent fewer inmates seventeen or younger. The biggest rise was in the oldest age group: an 85 percent increase in prisoners fifty-five or older. In the twenty to twenty-nine age group, historically most likely to be in prison, the rate of increase was about 22 percent. These figures suggest that the tide is turning, with incarceration rates for younger men and women rising more slowly than in the past.

The great challenge for Prison Fellowship and all who share its vision will be to continue reaching out to the culture, underscoring the cause-and-effect relationship between moral values and criminal behavior. Thirty years of ministry have shown that nothing is more self-destructive than moral relativity. Only a return to universally recognized moral standards will reduce crime, permit prison reform, and allow restorative justice, because without absolutes *crime, reform,* and *justice* mean whatever the one shouting the loudest says they do. Meaningful standards for mankind can be set only by a power higher and nobler than man.

There was no strategy, no objective at the beginning of the journey, only Chuck Colson's conviction that God was calling him to prison ministry and his willingness to be led. As Justice Fellowship president Pat Nolan said, "Chuck's a brilliant man, but at his cleverest he could not have designed this ministry the way God has."

What started in the wake of a presidential scandal thirty years ago has become a transforming cultural force not only behind prison walls but everywhere from the homes of ex-offenders to the halls of Congress. There's irony in the thought that the next great spiritual revival in America might well come from its cellblocks. While schools and courts battle over public expressions of faith and too many churches drift off into relativism, America's prisons ring with praise for Jesus Christ.

Notes

Chapter 1: Broken Vessels

1–8. Normal Morris and David J. Rothman, eds. *The Oxford History of the Prison: The Practice of Punishment in Western Society*. Rev ed. (Oxford: Oxford University Press, 1997), passim.

Chapter 2: Genesis

18. John Pierson, "Nixon's Hatchet Man: Call It What You Will, Chuck Colson Handles President's Dirty Work," *The Wall Street Journal*, October 15, 1971.

20–21. Charles W. Colson, *Born Again* (Revell, 1996), 14.

Chapter 3: A Vision in a Mirror

23. John Perry, *Charles Colson: A Story of Power, Corruption, and Redemption* (Nashville, TN: Broadman & Holman, 2003), 123–124.

25. C.S. Lewis, *Mere Christianity* (New York: HarperCollins, 2001), 122, 124.

31. Perry, *Charles Colson*, 203.

33–34. Charles W. Colson, *Life Sentence* (Grand Rapids: Fleming H. Revell, 1979), 40–41.

Chapter 4: Desperate Legacy

41–42. Scott Christianson, *With Liberty for Some: 500 Years of Imprisonment in America* (Boston: Northeastern University Press, 2000), 114, 119.

42–45. Normal Morris and David J. Rothman, eds. *The Oxford History of the Prison: The Practice of Punishment in Western Society*. Rev ed. (Oxford: Oxford University Press, 1997), 138–200.

46. Jessica Mitford, *Kind and Unusual Punishment* (New York: Vintage Books USA, 1964), 373. Gordon Hawkins, *The Prison: Policy and Practice* (Chicago: University of Chicago Press, 1976), 138.

Chapter 5: D. C. Disciples

57–59. Charles Colson, *Life Sentence* (Grand Rapids: Fleming H. Revell, 1979), 167, 209.

Chapter 6: Challenges Met

65–66. Charles Colson, *Life Sentence* (Grand Rapids: Fleming H. Revell, 1979), 210, 214.

73–74. Charles Colson, "Can Revival Save America?" *Jubilee* 5, no. 6 (July 1981): 2.

Chapter 7: God Behind Bars

81. Charles Colson, "Another Point of View" *Jubilee* 3, no. 3 (April 1979): 3.
82. Charles Colson, "Another Point of View" *Jubilee* 4, no. 6 (Aug. 1980): 1.
83. Steve Gettinger, "Informer," *Corrections Magazine* 4, no. 2 (April 1980): 17–19. Also quoted in Scott Christianson, *With Liberty for Some: 500 Years of Imprisonment in America* (Boston: Northeastern University Press, 2000), 274.
84–85. Christianson, *With Liberty for Some*, 274. See also Roger Morris, *The Devil's Butcher Shop: The New Mexico Prison Uprising*, rev ed. (Albuquerque, NM: University of New Mexico Press, 1988).
85–86. Charles Colson, "Another Point of View" *Jubilee* 4, no. 10 (Dec. 1980): 1.

Chapter 8: Molding the Message

89–90. Prison Fellowship, "PFM Volunteer In-Prison Certification Ministry Training Instructor Guide," Unpublished notebook.
91. Prison Fellowship, "Surviving and Thriving," Unpublished seminar booklet.
93. Interview by John Perry, Newton Correctional Facility, Newton, Iowa, February 14, 2005. Subject anonymous.

Chapter 9: On the Outside

103–104. See also Jane Willis, "Shedding Light on the Shadow of Death," *Jubilee* (June 1988): 1. By this time, *Jubilee* was indexed only by issue date.

Chapter 10: Remembering the Angels

115–116. *Prison Fellowship Presents Living Monuments* (Los Angeles, CA: The Shepherd Group. vol. 1, 1996. vol. 2, 1997), film.
120–123. Prison Fellowship Annual Report, 2004. Charles Colson and Mark Earley, eds. *Six Million Angels: Stories from 20 Years of Angel Tree's Ministry to the Children of Prisoners* (Ann Arbor, MI: Servant Publications, 2003), 50.

Chapter 11: Crime and Justice

127. Charles Colson, "Another Point of View," *Jubilee* 5, no. 1 (Jan. 1981): 94.
128–129. Lloyd C. Anderson, *Voices from a Southern Prison* (Athens, GA: University of Georgia Press, 2000), 84, 88.
130. Stanton Samenow and Samuel Yochelson, *The Criminal Personality* (New York: Jason Aronson, 1976). James Q. Wilson and Richard Herrnstein, *Crime and Human Nature* (New York: Simon & Schuster, 1985).
132–134. Charles Colson, "Another Point of View," *Jubilee* (May 1988): 7. Daniel W. Van Ness, "New Book by JF President," *The Justice Report* (Summer 1986): 5. See also Daniel W. Van Ness, *Crime and Its Victims* (Grand Rapids, MI: InterVarsity Press, 1986). Charles W. Colson, "Lessons of Pamela Small's Ordeal," *Washington Post*, May 12, 1989.

Chapter 12: Wilberforce Reformation

138. Interview with Charles W. Colson, Prison Fellowship Annual Report, 1991.
140. Abraham Kuyper, *Lectures on Calvinism* (Grand Rapids: MI: William B. Eerdman's, 1931), 27.
141. Charles W. Colson, "Foreword" in *Hero for Humanity: A Biography of William Wilberforce* (Colorado Springs, CO: NavPress, 2002), 12.
142–143. Kevin Belmonte, *Hero for Humanity*, 102, 137.

144–145. William Wilberforce, *Practical View of the Prevailing Religious System of Professed Christians in the Higher and Middle Classes in this Country Contrasted With Real Christianity* (1829; repr., Whitefish, MT: Kessinger Publishing, 2004), 9–10.

Chapter 13: Unto All the World

149–153. Gordon Loux, *Uncommon Courage: The Story of Prison Fellowship International* (Ann Arbor: MI, Servant Publications, 1987), 24–29.

157. Dean Ridings, "God's Unshakable Kingdom: Founded on Man's Weakness" *Jubilee* (Oct. 1986): 1.

Chapter 14: Coming of Age

170–173. Charles W. Colson, "The Enduring Revolution" (1993 Templeton Address delivered Sept. 2, 1993, at the University of Chicago, http://www.iclnet.org/pub/resources/text/cri/ENDREV-A.TXT).

Chapter 15: The Refiner's Fire

175–176. Charles W. Colson, Juan Diaz-Vilar, S.J., Avery Dulles, S.J., Francis George, OMI, Kent Hill, Richard Land, Larry Lewis, et al. "Evangelicals and Catholics Together: The Christian Mission in the Third Millennium" *First Things* 43 (May 1994): 15–22. Also available at http://www.firstthings.com/ftissues/ft9405/mission.html. Chuck W. Colson. Commenting on Evangelicals and Catholics Together. http://www.angelfire.com/ky/dodone/cc.html. Laurie Goodstein, "The 'Hypermodern' Foe; How the Evangelicals and Catholics Joined Forces," The Nation, *New York Times*, final ed., sec 4, May 30, 2004.

177. Charles W. Colson, interview by John Perry, August 18, 2005.

180–181. Charles W. Colson and Nancy Pearcey, "Introduction," in *How Now Shall We Live?* (Wheaton: Tyndale House Publishers, 1999), xii.

Chapter 16: Running the Race

190–191. Prison Fellowship, "Running the Race: A Bible-based 'Fitness Plan' for Your Life as a Christian." Unpublished title.

Chapter 17: Inner Change

198. *Encyclopaedia Britannica*, 15th ed., s.v. "Brazil."

203. Dan Kingery, interview with John Perry, Newton Correctional Facility, Newton, Iowa, February 15, 2005.

Chapter 18: James, Ron, and Matthew

206–209. James Corder, interview with John Perry, Newton Correctional Facility, Newton, Iowa, February 15, 2005.

209–212. Ron Gruber and Ken Lockhart, interviewed in *Prison Fellowship Presents Living Monuments* (Los Angeles, CA: The Shepherd Group. vol. 1, 1996. vol. 2, 1997), film.

212–218. Matthew Santamagro, interview with John Perry, Newton Correctional Facility, Newton, Iowa, February 15, 2005.

Chapter 19: The Next Chapter

222. Prison Fellowship 2004 Annual Report. Unpublished. *Prison Rape Elimination Act of 2003*, Public Law 108–79, 108th Cong., (Sept. 4, 2003) S. 1435 [108].